# The Last Word:
## Collected Poetry and Prose
## Volume 1 (1962-1976)

### by Ribitch

# The Last Word:
## Collected Poetry and Prose
## Volume 1 (1962-1976)

### by Ribitch

Oyster Moon Press
Berkeley, California

# The Last Word:
## Collected Poetry and Prose
## Volume 1 (1962-1976)
### by Ribitch

Any part of this book may be reproduced or transmitted
as long as credit is given to the author.
Copyright © 2019

ISBN: 978-0-578-22106-9

Additional copies of this book can be ordered from LuLu:
http://www.lulu.com

*Oyster Moon Press* is a non-profit, surrealist publishing co-op located in
Berkeley, California.

http://www.oystermoonpress.com

Dedicated to his mother, Marjorie, to his sister, Sandra, to his loving wife, Dorlene, to his sons, David and Jason, to his friend and collaborator, Eric Bragg, and to the global Surrealist community.

# Contents:

Forword ................................................................. 1

1960s .................................................................... 3

1970 ................................................................... 11

1971 ................................................................... 31

1974 ................................................................... 61

1975 ................................................................. 117

1976 ................................................................. 223

# Forword

What do you do with a man who feels deeply, who will not turn his face and pretend he just doesn't see? Here before you is the work of a man who did just that, a man who saw it all and continued, steadfastly loyal to the power of his own imagination.

*Things are what they are and what we make them
And we are what we make ourselves.\**

A prophet, possibly, a chronicler of the social era he lived in, certainly. A Surrealist, or as Franklin Rosemont once said of him, "Ribitch is surreal." He spent his life creating and living in his own reality. His work springs from deep within his psyche, automatic and uncensored. He never refined or reworked a piece, rather always allowed it to stand naked in the world for all to see.

*So be what you will, but be it well
And who should say,
What it is,
How it is
Or where it is.\**

Ribitch's earliest encounter with Surrealism began with the work of Salvador Dalí and expanded quickly as he read more about the philosophy, including the work of André Breton and other early Surrealists. In November of 1975 he came across a copy of *Arsenal/ Surrealist Subversions*, which contained an appeal by Phillip Lamantia, seeking like minds on the west coast. His response to that appeal led to a meeting with the San Francisco Surrealist group later that winter. There he learned of a World Surrealist Exhibition: *Marvelous Freedom, Vigilance of Desire*, organized by the Arsenal group in Chicago, set to open at Gallery Black Swan the following year. He attended that exhibition where, among many others, he met Franklin and Penelope Rosemont, Robert Green and Deborah Taub. In the winter of 1977-78 he returned to Chicago and participated in

1

the International Surrealist Exhibition: *One Hundredth Anniversary of Hysteria*, in Cedarburg, Wisconsin in the spring of 1978.

Over the years he stayed in communication with the International Surrealist Movement, and with the advent of the internet, he was able to communicate and collaborate with surrealist comrades around the world. In 2008, he and Eric Bragg cofounded Oyster Moon Press in Berkeley, California, where, most notably, he was one of the editors that produced two editions of *HYDROLITH*, a journal of Surrealist research and investigations.

His commitment to the "emancipation of the imagination" took many forms: poetry, visual arts, music, and storytelling. Wherever he went, he was street theater. At every opportunity, he took time to encourage and mentor children using stories, theater games, automatic writing, and drawing in a social as well as an educational setting.

Ribitch literally created hundreds of pieces of visual art in many different forms. He always immersed himself in each new media completely until a new one caught his interest. He was never without his sketch book in which he wrote and drew daily.

I invite you to laugh, cry, be repulsed, bowled over, and amazed by the work of a man who inspired me to live through my imagination; a man I am happy to have had the opportunity to spend a great deal of time with, and to call a friend.

Sharon Olson

---

*Cited from poem, "But Who Should Say", page 5 of this volume.

1960's

*Ribitch: The Last Word, Volume 1*

## BUT WHO SHOULD SAY!

Beware of him,
who stands in the dark corners,
sipping wine through a silver-plated straw,
and he who smokes marijuana with a cigarette holder,
for he is the one who grows, older, and colder.
A crust of dirt forms upon the window sill,
only to be blown away again,
with the slight gusts of wind.
But who should say,
what it is,
how it is,
or where it is.

In walks the crownless king,
behind him walks the breastless queen.
to sit upon the throne of nothingness;
Then in flutters the jester with his bells all a jingle, a jingle, a jangle...
"Hail ye king",
then he gets to his knees, to weep about the long forgotten Joan of Arc,
But who should say,
what it is,
how it is,
or where it is.

Then the king looks down on him,
as if he was a pauper, gazing into the den of riches.
Then the gaze changes,
and his stare becomes a flaming torch of hell.
"Dear king, I am what I am,"
pleaded the jester, "and nothing more".
Then he cried once, twice, and then a third.
But who should say,
what it is,
how it is,
or where it is.

*1960s*

Scholars gather, and followers mourn,
another great genius has bitten the dust.
He lies in his gilded coffin, so white
so cold, so deathly pale,
O' but why, why must things be so?
Things are what they are and what we make them.
And we are what we make ourselves.
But who should say,
what it is,
how it is,
or where it is.

The knight with all his armor walks,
very slowly he walks, bogged down by the weight.
He looks so gallant and so brave.
But when he steps out he's nothing
but a skinny old man, with no teeth.
The wickedness is drained out of his wrinkled body.
To be restored by a new form, jealousy, the root of evil.
But who should say,
what it is,
how it is,
or where it is.

The world is ours; it is how we make it,
and nothing more,
we are ourselves and nothing more.
The man with wine and silver straw,
the crownless king, the weeping jester,
they are what they make of themselves,
and nothing more.
So be what you will, but be it well.
And who should say,
what it is,
how it is,
or where it is.


Unknown date 1966

## THE ROCK

Rock, o' little rock,
        sit, sit, and still sit,
till someone comes to pick you up
and fling you to the far horizon.
Rock, o' little rock,
        nobody cares for you.
You're just a solid mass...
You're a rock,
        nothing but a rock.


Unknown date 1966

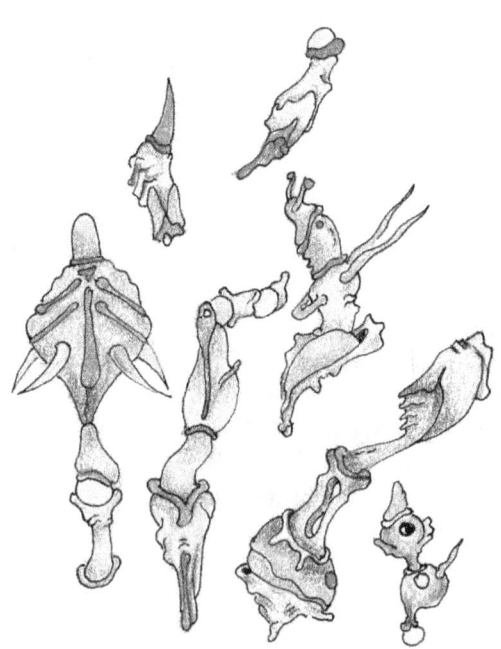

*1960s*

**VISIONS OF EXPECTANT**

I leaned against the wall
Trying to gather myself,
But I'm now gone too far from what is real
I can't come down.
I take it easy as it comes,
And I'm hungry and insane.
All the sexless people
They just stand around and boast
About their secret hideaways.
All of our sins aren't sins,
We just blame ourselves
For what's wrong.
The dust forms on the empty wine bottles,
I haven't shaved,
And I can't accept myself.
But it's a shame anyway about the war
I must put it down for the sake of my own mind.
Silence was broken by sounds of music,
Stoned two weeks...
My mind went paranoid,
I was lost in the pain in here,
I just can't sit
I must move....
After smoking
Inhale and the world is free of hate.
Tricks played on my mind


Unknown date 1966

*Ribitch: The Last Word, Volume 1*

## SOLITUDE

To the fleeting moments of solitude in vacuum mirror eyes,
and there I sit in frozen mind made up of solitude smiles in pools of roses.
So I'll just sit in solitude, thinking of the vacuum and its hallways,
eating bone-meal cookies, reading magazines, watching television,
and just growing older, to become so much wiser by using a brand-name shaver,
And looking into the mirror to see the same old face,
as it stares back at me, with closed eyes and retracted mind.

Through the flowing fog I sit thinking, and will be there always,
just to count the flowers that grow by the river.
I am counting the stars at night.
Maybe I should give lessons on sitting silently rocking.
Solitude is empty, as the flesh upon my body.
There I shall be empty, and taken far from the city
to a place where I can think out my solitude.
A place to hide my insanity or maybe a place to do some thinking.
Thinking about neon, plastic clouds that never seem to disappear,
waters that never evaporate, drums that never end and perfume smells that never stop.

The children wrapped up in the arms of their mothers, are taken up with care by their fathers,
Neither loved by God nor the world, but grown old by the solitary times.
I had better start thinking, or maybe start contemplating, because the night is short,
And my pockets are empty with no change to call home bail.
I see a wheelchair aging in the sun with no one to sit in it,
and me sitting there thinking that maybe I'll go and sit in it and howl at the moon.
The stars fade in the night and I just sit here thinking about doctors, and politicians,
project houses, authorities, and the twisted angles of highrise monoliths.

I wish to go to the green fields forever, not to be lost in this hell of city vibrations.
My predestined death already planned and the tickets are sold out.
To be the pawn, now for a moment a king, a king without a crown, a king without a throne.
When does the night end? Never, no never, still never, and infinity.

*1960s*

To be drunk in love, and living with time.
I am the Joker in the deck. It is sad that *time* begs to nobody.
But we win, by begging to time that love will conquer war.
Who will come? Not I! Who will go? Not I.
My moods are torn apart by distractions, of this and that.
I can't quit, no it's no use... I can't stop; no it's no use...
Untouched by time? Not I.

Unknown date 1966

1970

## A CITY'S PLAY

Beach love,
thin light hung above my head.
All night wine-drinking
with street shouts that crack my ears,
in long-lasting drones of propeller screams.
Later I am lying drunk upon my bed
with sad erection staring at pale wall.
Rat-dung closet floors,
where hours were spent in yellow stains,
that of stale smoke.
Thirty fuckers beneath my bed,
making squeals of exotic horns,
that never stop in the street below.

On feeling lonely,
I walk three blocks to downtown movie house
and pay my fare to see whores being laid in 3-D,
but I fall asleep with my fingers
netted gently in my long knotted hair.
There, beneath moving starlets,
with naked, pig-breath smiles.
Brown nipples big as the state of Texas,
I slept with all the things that I fear
beneath my seat.
Tomorrow's bus,
from downtown slums to uptown hustlers,
bathroom cronies of stale whiskey-breath
that calls me as I pass
with long searching fingers.

Rich laughter, cracked mirrors,
love letters on toilet walls,
and the smell of urine washbasins and
old powdered soap.
Sailor's laughter, bus station clatter,
the pinball machine marking up points
to the lady laughing, sticking her finger to the button,
ball flying to score the last and losing point.
Stepping into night air,
pumping muscles,
legs moving slowly up sidewalks,
a white sea of cement.

*1970*

Taxi, Taxi,
running shouts of hurried husbands,
returning from office day labor.
Eight hour heart attacks,
with briefcase saddle sores and black tie collar burns.
Taxi, Taxi.
Catching breath, time for highball ulcer cramps,
doctor tests, cancered brain of
run home read the latest sad news
(Joe in black and white)
to then turn to frozen T.V. to hear
announcers tell you what you read.
Sidewalk sea rising and falling,
running in squares.
parallel,
across and dead-end,
with lights red, yellow, green,
Walk, don't walk,
interrupting patterns of trained human thinking,
with sidewalk seas
hungry for feet of drowning pedestrians,
walking past lighted store window fronts,
of slyly gazing at ladies' behinds,
thinking of how round it is under her tight knit skirt.

Reflections of self
staring blankly at naked mannequins
with wild, unsleeping eyes that glitter like fires
beneath tall lighted buildings,
rising higher every day
till it chokes the sky,
till it chokes the clouds,
till it chokes finally the moving figures below,
waiting for light changes,
listening to horns and tires screeching,
cussing drivers yelling their "fuck you"
in the crisp night air.
Lifting fist and fingers like rising flags
to show the world their pride and honor,
to be part of the streets,
garbage-pail existence;
darting into dim lighted bars.
Hearing always Hank William's country drawl
and beer-soaked memories of love lost,

only lost, for nothing ever seems to be gained.
With noses stuck deep in tall glasses,
old friends clapping hands,
buying drinks,
buying time,
selling out,
selling out.

A lot of everything out there
frozen into frowning faces,
reflecting in eyes
as cold icecubes tinkling at the bottom of glasses.
No cherry,
no fruit of vine,
no stationary door to walk through,
no beacon light out of the fog
shining deeply into pools of living lust.
All this, stained there on my sheets,
mingling with the sweat clinging to my body,
which is trembling in deep psychotic trance,
which is naked between my thoughts,
which is all frozen within me.
It is etched there in the form of wash basins.
toilet seats and a statue of Voltaire,
whose nose shows white in window sun,
whose aged brow stands wrinkled in wasted harmony,
whose last words were spoken trough plaster eyes.
I stand on my trembling legs,
walking feebly to filthy window glass,
staring at the city's glare.

I peer out with reaching hands
that grab at the sun with calloused fingers,
feeding warmth across my face,
warmth that seems to erase away my fears
that I may have stored up in tiny glass thoughts,
warmth that comforts me on Forty-Second Avenue
beneath strung clothing
and jabbering old ladies
talking of neighbors, how much prices are rising
on everything from corner vegetables to street junk.
Remarkable old ladies with junk-filled arms,
with junk-filled minds,
with junk-filled souls,

## 1970

and with the will to sell their bodies to drunk and horny sailors
with just enough change to buy a broken piece.
Flies encircle environmental crises
waiting to devour human need,
to become soul survivors of a barren street desert
where nothing is left but empty shops,
blaring out last phonographs for no ears to hear.

Downstairs and into the street hot with the sun,
eyes that burn from brown-tinted air,
going through magnificent lungs that are chocked up
with so many cinders of burning industries.
Industrial boom
to create many dollars,
to buy coffins for lung-less, eyeless misfortunes
of the great American waste.
The eagle without a voice to screech,
the eagle without destiny or a nation to claim,
he is a fallen stone beneath the feet
of running, trembling madmen
Whose only concern is with the lumpy brown wallets
that pad their asses,
that conquer their spirits.
This is the street I endlessly plod,
feet sinking in dry cement,
wandering from hole to hole.

This is the street I must greet morning after morning
till noon's hottest sun
that raises atop brick monuments to dollar gods.
Hot cement hollows
where caves hide dwellers in sorrowful hate,
where too many lonely fire escapes tower over
black asphalt human emotions,
where my feet tread on endless miles of everyday.
Crossing over my crossovers
again and again
till my brain wilts in summer's heat.
Later I burst forward as a gigantic orgasm,
throwing off old chains,
and walk up blind streets,
entering spasms of the city's play.

Unknown date 1970

**BOTTOM**

Fingers stop, angry touch
eyes glazed in graveyard gray
stooped over trashcan heaps.
Hungry stomach pains in evil noise,
with groans of days stretched.
Tincan rolling across smiles
of bread found.
Hungry fingers searching
long glances into dark caverns
of pails and bins.
Perilous adventures of alleyways
search for thoughtful food
to sustain life's pitiful existence.
Bottom, glance and a scrape.
Fingers stop, angry touch.


Unknown date 1970

*1970*

**ELEGIA**

Night,
on robes of red,
and webs of silken silver,
throughout the iron steed,
it rose,
higher, and higher.
Glass eyes,
or the turning point,
of the flags
that wave,
they fall
like broken petals
in frozen water.
In cellophane space,
no fingers touch
the soft bottoms
of sweet taste,
or laughing boys
in their masculinity
pregnant with guilt,
in flowing Madness.
In turned around
rubber faced mama,
a finger
that twisted
and shot out
like a bull of Spain,
and it becomes
ink upon the wall,
bulging as night,
A night with no eyes,
A night without tomorrow.
Flaming, grinning,
Pointing out the mistakes,
letting them rise
in moral context.
Bulging eyes, blue-faced
in mockery,
underlying breath,
With indulgence aware,
the voice that fades
in the webs of today,

in the night.

The cold abyss
of the unloving sky is
unfolding.

Unknown date 1970

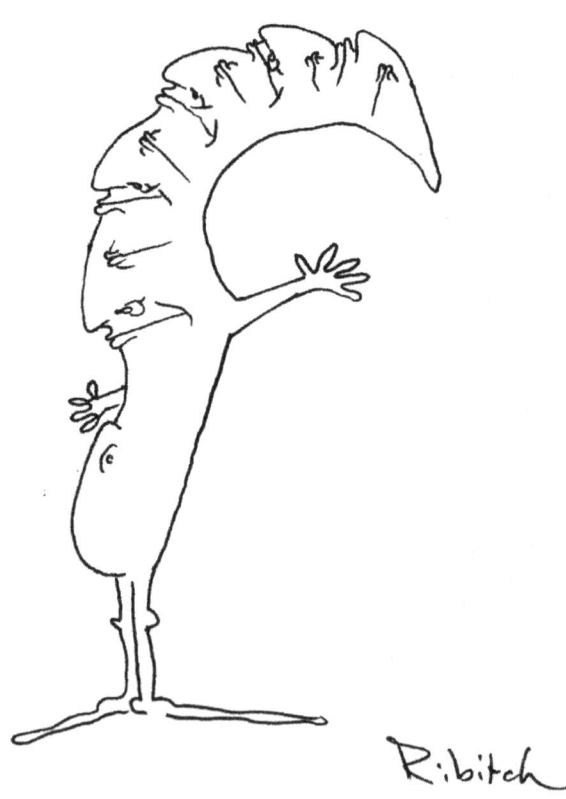

*1970*

## FRESH UPON THE WINDOWSILL (UNTITLED)

Fresh upon the windowsill
the glassy dew fell,
like many diamonds falling
into crystal dreams.
Laughing, weeping there,
the frost fell on my feet
as I sat hitchhiking,
cold, and numb, was I,
too sad for it to bother,
sadness upon me seeking
for home, and love.
I waited, but was broken.
The world was just a dream
to follow down the road,
wide in the utmost misery.
I lay upon the ground
and then began to cry,
for what was so long ago,
that my eyes could no longer see.
The stars were above me
telling me a tale,
of a lonely gypsy wife
that lost her child in death.
So sad, that my fingers
clutched my head in fright.
Sadness that held me to its breast
and my tears they fell in scores.
The love that she held
was so familiar and true.
I straighten my head up to the sky,
and prayed for just one chance,
to love again without the hurt
that comes when it dies.

Unknown date 1970

**ONE INTO ONE**

One into one,
into the other,
both into two,
the two into four,
positive,
ultra-positive,
positive,
ultra-positive,
the one to make the
three,
less counted
the two,
sub-positive,
or negative,
positive being
independent of
changing circumstances
or relations,
while the negative
proceeds oppositely
to an arbitrary positive
direction.
This is to be
existence and nonexistence.


Unknown date 1970

*1970*

## ROLL OUT BETWEEN YOUR FINGERS (UNTITLED)

Roll out,
slid between your fingers,
be that quick glance,
and follow that thin snake.
Make way for lasting music,
gleaming
past shadows,
ducking under lights.
Between the glass carnations,
emotions,
silver clouds,
and memories.
Loving the flowing highway
leading on past
the yellow fields,
past yellow sun,
past pale existence
of blue flowing sky.
Lifting feet above
dusty roads below me,
laughing at the sunset
above me.
Making like a summer's wind,
letting my fingers touch
the hill beside me.
piercing my body
with the rushing tide
of day coming.


12/11/ 70

## TALKING OF...

A quest in free-flowing
        ladies talking
rows across rivers,
sighing at heavenly bodies
        Of rich
            bureaucratic widows,
whose only relief comes to mind
after dinner movies
of great detest and horror,
of rape,
thriller,
spellbinder.
The egg is finally broken,
to hatch the human beings
that pick hungrily
at each other
for something to fill their needs.
A gothic picture
of souls licking their fingers,
and their lips,
laughing humorously
at their reflections.

Unknown date 1970

*1970*

**THE OLDS 88**

Miss Ann walked to the terrace
her skin cold, cold white,
and she gazed to the driveway,
upon the Olds 88.
The wind blew in circles,
the leaves withered brown,
blew around her hair,
and brushed across her feet.
That was the last true emotion
that came to my heart,
as she spread her fingers,
closed her eyelids,
and let space become her child.
I let my voice linger
in the cold thin air,
Ann, Miss Ann,
my soul belongs to you,
in fire next to your breast.
My eyes followed
as she became an angel of blue.
She turned and smiled,
her teeth
fluorescent white,
hardly visible.
She raised a finger to her lips,
as if to hush the
sound of wind.
As her head tilted back,
a piercing scream
split the air.
Then...
the air was empty,
and space lingered on
the terrace.
The wind stopped,
the leaves fell still,
and the Olds 88
crumbled like dried clay
beneath my feet.

"Alpha", Miss Ann cried.
 Her body could not be seen,

her shadows now almost gone.
"Beginnings," was the next voice called
Miss Ann's, though weak and lost.
I could hear her cries,
the wails of a dying dog.
I could feel the touch
of her eyes blazing
death in tormented rages
through my soul.
If space once took,
Hell on calloused knees,
her flesh, like flame
licked at my face.
I could feel her wrath,
and smell her presence near.
"Barthelme, questionable liaison
with your tin models,
and the deaths
in whiffs of marble stone,
for all the young men
that died beneath your iron foot."
Miss Ann spoke to me
in hatred.
My body began to cringe,
my tongue began to swell.
My skin began to feel
the sticky slime of sweat.
I could feel the electric touch
of Miss Ann's fingers
clutch my thought,
as light pierced my thoughts.
A soft hum of angels
creased the air,
and I began to gag and vomit
while fingers grew tighter
in the vice-like grip.
I screamed, but no voice was there,
I began to fling my arms
wildly in the air,
at empty space.
In darkly princes
the dust-ravished soul
indigo walls
holding

*1970*

holding
the dust-ravished soul.
I cried, like a baby,
strangled by blue ribbon.
The moon was flowing
past me, and I knew...
I knew...
The wolves that came
to embark upon me,
also came to...
I screamed and panic sticks
to my heart.
I can feel her presence
crushing me,
she...entered me,
became a part of my flesh.
Her eyes became space,
that encircled me.
I don't think I could
sing love songs.
Fiery flames engulf
my house,
my yard,
my heart.
Today, today, today, today,
I've got to shout today,
because tomorrow my tongue
may be fragmented by her words.
Scream.

I AM DEAD!

M-I-S-S  A-N-N  D-R-A-G  M-E  A-W-A-Y

Such a fool I've been,
about it all.
Why?
I wish it was all over with.

I am a dead fish.
I am a dead horse.
I am a dead moth.
I am a dead man.

## Ribitch: The Last Word, Volume 1

Such a small person I am,
that all the sky smothers me.
The bell,
it rings.
The tower must have someone in it.
The bell can't ring itself.
"Miss Ann, let me..."
Bells, bells,
I walk to the tower,
the bells continued to ring.
The stairs wound on to the top,
where in the darkness
was nothing.
Bells that ring themselves?
Good lord, what's happening here?
The bells continued to ring.
Louder, and louder,
till my ears began to burst.
I held my hands to my head,
the rush of adrenaline
spun me dizzy.
The works of the clock
fell still.
I glanced out of the tower window,
to see a Greyhound bus,
filled with sickly people.
Escaping northbound,
through the fog of emotions.
Their skin is gray and placid,
their eyes cold, white.
They turn their heads
and their lips spread
the smiles,
of the hate they bore.
All the evilness
encased in motionless souls
began its pitiful groans.

Dead?
Such an odd word.
I am...
Plentiful eyes
that stretch the outward existence,
and play with tiny fingers.

*1970*

Dead,
and not so holy.

Spark,
that ember of lust,
a broken mind.
Shattered, like broken glass,
tiny pieces.

WHITE!

Unholy, moral understanding, that last walk.
That last walk, understanding last breath, and understanding.

DAYBREAK!

White clouds that rise above all other existences.
A final cheer from the crowd.

SUNRISE!

Immoral gratitudes,
my mind waves,
are in no
metrical pattern.
A falsehood in my existence.

DEATH!

I think I know, at last.
Transcending, Miss Ann.
Transcending through…
through
a piercing scream,
that wails in my thoughts,
for the realization
that I don't know
what it is I'm transcending through.
Misery unfolds down here
in the darkness.
Down here?
Why…
down here.
No other reason to be

anything else,
but down here.

THEIVES!

The night is red,
all blood that spared the sky.
Human waste,
the Olds 88,
the vanishing dreams.
Dirt, all that dirt,
that sticks to my eyelids.
Hell, Miss Ann,
Hell.
A place you prescribed.
A dead, wretched place,
do you hear me?
A dead wretched place.
Hell,
your outer covering
has been removed.
Unholy, unrest,
the candle has been snuffed.

WHITE!
DAYBREAK!
SUNRISE'S DEATH!

Yes I think I know at last.
And as my smile too became the air,
I could feel the cold of the terrace.
My eyes burned from the wind,
watching, watching,
the Olds 88
disappears down the road.


Unknown date 1970

*1970*

## THE STONE OF ARTTY GABLE

Long time ago, under the sand, raised the stone of Artty Gable,
with the lamp-lighted rose petal gliding gently to the pond,
where liver willy pea frogs play at the water's edge.
Glass sailing ships, sparkled suns upon the water's lips,
and a song of green wood, water beetles skip off into moss-tinted wine,
And there is, to be sure, the stone of Artty Gable
beneath the throne of moss wood pine,
where also lies the golden braid,
where also lie the coins of thought,
where also lies the human heart, bleeding out love as red as blood,
which covered a million tiny fireflies dancing in the green of the moon.
It was a splendid evening to be underneath a log watching races.
Grasshoppers and bees,
oh, to fly that fast,
piercing air, piercing rainbow flowers, pinks and greens.
Yellow flower petal, stealing rings beneath the flow of dancing bears,
whose flip-flops upon painted clouds make me laugh inside my tummy,
sending grins to other parts of the world.
It's so nice to be greeted by a million butterflies
all singing politely upon one drop of dew,
leaning out touching the love between them.
Radiant and ghostly alive, the stone of Artty Gable,
with its painted symbols of heaven and earth.
Shielded by seven stars, and dimmed by the years,
it was all the light they had.
But we could see the horizon, covered in soft emerald greens.
Candle wax and aphrodisiac wind, the world softly croons.
Lightly prancing upon silver strands was Gregory Mouse, the alchemist,
and round the stone of Artty Gable,
sitting beneath the throne of moss wood pine,
letting fingers gently touch,
letting tongues mingle and collide
like a thousand suns' thundering crystals of broken glass and waves of cool air.
Again, about the stone,
the eyeglass fitted properly between the folds of the king's left eye,
who blinked the sigh of relief, drank pure bread wine,

and danced with all the glowworms.
The holy prince lay naked in the shadow of the stone of Artty Gable,
teardrop eyes gave light into deep caverns,
deep eyes, deep holy cinders, burnt of lifers flesh.
Rings out of the sky, is a blank reminder of empty hearts
coldly mingled with fingertips.
Blue laced lips and those deep eyes,
staring at liver willy pea frogs, groundhogs,
and talisman of different colors.
Moldy Mold with outstretched hands,
a grin that stretched from ear to ear,
and eyebrows were plucked of every hair.
He is standing, where?
Upon the stone of Artty Gable,
head held high, first into blue denim sky,
and being swallowed ever slowly,
Under the throne of moss wood pine.
It is swallowed ever slowly into the stone of Artty Gable,
though we're mad in tower's prison,
chained and barred from freely choosing to watch.
The bears joyfully dancing,
or how the sailing ships exploded into thousands of tiny bells,
ringing songs of happy birds,
gentle flow of running water,
sunlight peering above the pond giving new laughter,
but hot upon the stone of Artty Gable,
that has cracked all its evil,
born the man of spears and arrows
from the stone of Artty Gable.


Unknown date 1970

1971

## ALFRED IN WAITING

Past paranoid glimpses of street
Laughter,
Caught by the balls,
Hung like lamp light,
Above chatter,
Clatter,
A thousand searching
Fingers,
Probing the self-search,
Like old ladies
Laughing, cunt twitter,
With their fingers
Stuck between their legs,
In search of tiny men
Who might be hiding
From Neo-Nazi-Commie
Ameriken eagle shit
That twitters their feathers
At pocketbooks,
For money screams,
Of raising taxes
For useless wars,
That drags on endless
Years, of dead boys,
That makes fathers proud,
Like Ameriken flag,
Stained red,
Blood,
For a country
That doesn't give a damn,
Because it died,
And no one wants
To admit it,
In fear that they might
Lose their fat cars,
Their plush automatic
Ass wipers,
And two-hundred years
Of goddamn glory.

June 28, 1971

*1971*

**ALFRED**

Alfred, with the moan in the night,
Screaming: shiftless moods,
Walking the streets,
Like a thousand years
Of minds that resemble
Lepers dying forever
In the pits of the city's groan.
Alfred, who died
Like the rest,
With his eyes blind from hate and greed.
With the wind in his hair,
With his fear beneath his pillow
Like the lions in his mind,
That torture and pull at his soul.
Alfred, the weak,
The politician,
The pimp,
The geek.
Alfred, with voice
That spills out lies
Like flowing rivers,
Continuous stream of faces.
Lies like the scream of night,
The wail of police cars,
Picking a thousand ears to hear,
A thousand eyes to see,
Like lips that move with no words.
Alfred, helpless
The height of his career,
A beggar,
On the steps of his wealthy home.


Unknown date 1971

**AMERICA I SAW YOU DIE**

I listen with my eyes,
To silent deaths on unfamiliar streets,
Past Coca Cola, Foster Freeze,
Cadillac, wine bottle,
no face alley, dying trenches,
You America have made me paranoid!
Lies, school book history
America I see you...
I have seen you before
madness in your television sets,
mortuary with dying palms,
empty buildings,
statues of grand and glorious men
standing guard over citified mummies,
dying in sanitariums,
lost in San Francisco,
broken in some bar off the road,
shivering in some hotel toilet,
caught with your shorts down,
screaming that the dime you earned
at fourteen is still hanging above your wall,
Who gives a shit?
I ask you,
and you tell me,
and you weep at words that could not
make it past your lips.
You died last week,
and I saw it happen,
You were blown away in a political storm,
you tried hard though,
but finally you flickered
and went out like a flame.


Unknown date 1971

*1971*

**BALCONY EYEBALLS**

Staring off indefinitely, chattering above storefronts,
watching the day pass, like waiting for trains in empty stations.
Television set minds, gazing off into the city's wail,
where the screams of everyday street robots go on like mature mutations,
grinning a moral belief, while scratching their asses.
They take their dope, like old ladies sampling fish at the market,
with their toothsome grins, and their bad breath, and their holy cross.
They go to church every Sunday
for the sake of eating the little crackers and grape juice.
The park across the street with its boys in tight pants,
who grin with endless glances at ass, and cocks,
and then they run in and out of toilet stalls blushing slightly,
screaming to be had. And mindless freaks are dancing around trees,
talking to the shrubs, being calmly surreal in the warm afternoon.


5/ 27/71

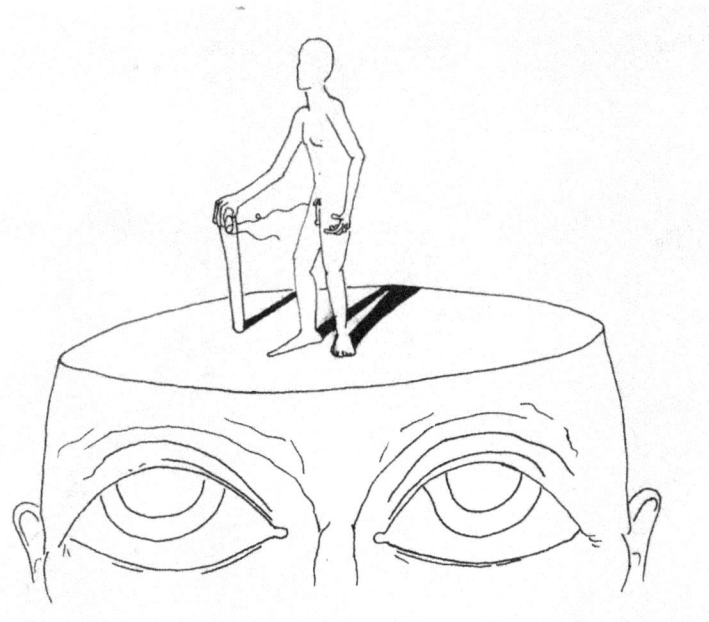

*Ribitch: The Last Word, Volume 1*

**BURNING THE SYMBOLS OF A NATION**

Speaking for a world that needs a state of mind, or a course of action to solve its problems, while people are singing "America the Beautiful" with their heads in a paper bag. Being unable to breath, in the filth they themselves possess. How they shout how clean and nice they are, using their mouth as a filtering system for the shit their brains put out. "Stand in line, get your hands out of your pockets," shouts the great wind. "You're going to get it right or I'll beat your head in". You're trying to be quiet, but the voice is already caught in your throat, "Gasp!"

The hallway is full of bodies trying to sleep, when the shepherd of salvation with his jellyfish smile shouts for God and country, and shows you a medal he got for shooting a faggot during the war. How brave he must have been, put behind a desk of thieves, when in reality it was that man with the stop sign nailed to his forehead who was to blame. For he knew the law but didn't try to stop it, but stuck a knife into her plump naked body, lifted his head and cried, "liberty", and he kissed her bosom and wept, "conform to me, you silly bitch".

Unknown date 1971

*1971*

**DON'T SAY LOVE**

Love,
Is it an easier word to say
Now that you've laid down your flowers?
Love,
Is it an easier word to say
With a Molotov cocktail in your hand?
Love,
Roll it around in your mouth
Mix it with the blood of your hate.
Love,
Is it an easier word to say?

All of your kisses have turned to shouts,
Don't say love!
The flowers have turned to guns,
Don't say love!
Your music has turned to war chants,
Don't say love!

Don't say love,
My father still calls black man nigger.
Don't say love,
When war still rages in Viet Nam.
Don't say love,
While the banks are burning.
Don't say love,
After you say revolution.
Don't say love,
And use the word with murder.
Don't say love,
And shoot a policeman.
Don't say love,
Like Timothy Leary.
Don't say love,

Don't say love,
That's not your word,
Don't say love,
With that gun at my head.
Don't say love,
Until you're ready to believe it,
Don't say love,

## Ribitch: The Last Word, Volume 1

Until you're ready to use it,
Don't say love,
Without taking your brother's hand
And saying it together.
Because it does not mean a thing unless you believe in it.

April 26 1971

*1971*

## HIDEOUS HANNA

A million square inches of Hideous Hanna, her fat ponderous female beast.
She is a continuous sea of obesity, rolls, upon rolls, folds upon folds.
Her navel can't be seen and her breasts flow from her like watermelon jelly.
Her face puckers out wanting lust in thick inviting lips.
Her tongue curls, her eyes squint,
and she shakes her wide waist, letting everything spill and flow.
What excitement she holds between her legs, cannot be seen for the
expanding thighs,
that shimmers, and throbs, that invites a closer look, feel, or taste.
The round of her buttocks, when bent to spread, is like an enormous
catcher's mitt.
If you want more than just a ball, but arms that could hold you,
To crush you in their wanting squeeze, and draw you in to be lost,
in the rolls of her skin, where no one could find you in a million years.
And when at last, the laughter, and climax has ended, the fat turns to butter,
the butter turns to butterfly wings, and a million square inches,
of Hideous Hanna, rise and roll out of the room, bouncing the nakedness of
her
Continuous form...


Unknown date 1971

*Ribitch: The Last Word, Volume 1*

**HOWDY IS ALIVE**

I have heard
Howdy Doody is alive,
In the mind of Buffalo Bob,
Arisen from the dust
Of past years,
Peanut gallery,
And tears of
Joy and happiness...
"What time is it boys and girls?"
It's time to wake
Out of our dreams.
"It's Howdy Doody time."
It's time for lunch,
And Clarabell Clown,
Silent majority,
Always wanting
To cut the strings,
And let Howdy fall,
With a wooden thud
To the stage below.
I hear Buffalo Bob Is alive,
In the mind of Howdy Doody,
Escaping now on the run
To recapture the enlightened years,
Away from the paranoia
Of a dying world,
Escaping to a last stage,
A last peanut gallery,
Filled with screaming children
Born too late for the pleasure,
Of Howdy's smile.
I hear America is alive,
In the mouths of children shouting,
"It's Howdy Doody time."
Again, and again
Till it shakes the walls
Of congress, and the war department,
And enters the streets, With laughter and joy.
"What time is it boys and girls?"
Time to shake
Off the dust... "It's Howdy Doody time."


June 23 1971

*1971*

## I THINK I CAN SET THE BLAME NOW

Amongst the endless walls
the dead torn curtains,
and the beeping, honking scream
that seems to never end below,
where eyes are faintly shut
in the gray afternoon dust.
The city's rectum,
spewing out lives,
that horrible living dung.
human society,
The clamor of all the wealth
and intelligence, and some ridiculous
thing called common sense.
      MANKIND,
the heap,
the sweet heap,
the marvelous all-knowing heap,
the thinking heap,
the sewer,
with the mind that does nothing,
out to adjust itself to filth.
and parades, to glorify heroes,
with confetti,
Gray clouds of falling paper,
Blowing across miles
of boulevards and avenues,
covering the naked stench of gutter alleyways,
and half-dead winos
asleep in the parks.
The parks, the place for beauty
recreation, and for children,
the parks, now, dark with fear
and murder,
and the smell of wine and sweat,
and filled with sobs of young girls
parted beneath the spreading willows.
the sky to be dark,
for the spreading arms of human heap.
And the only peace there is,
Is slowly being muffled out.

Unknown date 1971

## JOSEPH IN HAMMER NAIL
**(Poem to Joseph McCarthy)**

Joseph in paranoia,
afraid of grave robbers, who might be communist,
Sneaking into his coffin, to corrupt his moral Amerikan way of life.
Joseph in eternal fallout shelter,
hiding from...
What it was, that he thought he knew?
It drew his breath,
gutted his life,
and laid him away, in fear of every Russian diplomat,
that shook his hand, or that he found hiding beneath his bed.
Joseph the Amerikan eagle, the saint of fear.
Joseph in paranoia,
Joseph in the minds of war babies everywhere.


May 30 1971

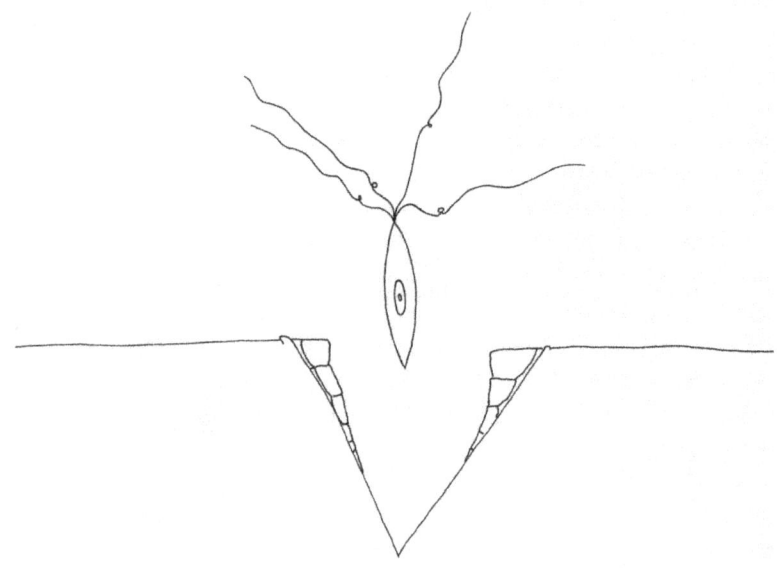

*1971*

**MECHANICAL LUST**

Practicing restraint,
Like sticking your head in the mud,
With all the mechanical doodads,
That go,
> Click, clack,
> Flip, flop,
> Ding, dong

And robot people,
Slaves to the industrial rage.
Counting on their electric counters,
What they could count on their fingers,
And their eyes that flash,
At new and wonderful things that go,
> Click, clack,
> Flip, flop,
> Ding, dong

Like television sets,
Taking over the world,
With brainwash commercials
For cars, and trash-smashers,
And electric ass-wipers,
And more doodads, That go,
> Click, clack,
> Flip, flop,
> Ding, dong

That create more minds
Indignant to the world,
Outside of the button, switch,
And telephone cord

May 27 1971

## NOISY DAYS

It just seemed to be
another one of those
noisy days,
lost in the drones
of talking people,
waving lips,
flashing tongues,
with endless streams
of candy words,
that go on and on
till they hit the wall
and shatter.
Pieces fall around my ears:
talk, screams, laughter,
words that fall apart
and fall into coffee cups,
alphabet soup,
floating in the air
past my eyes,
past the open mouths,
colliding into molded words
then mixing inside me,
till finally my voice too
is lost in the clouds of noisy days.

Unknown date 1971

*1971*

## POEM FOR ALLEN GINSBERG

eye, see
charisma follower,
and holy man,
flower petal
tongue
flashing out ohm's
peaceful existence
laying
beneath suns
becoming
the earth,
the eye.
of love,
the soul
of life,
a follower
of energy,
a leader
of energy.
eye,
see you
like a sun
rising
to a new day


Jan 24, 1971

## POOR ALFRED

Maybe it was Alfred who sat on the city council, complaining about the over suited budget, and bad coffee. Only my forgotten brothers that sat muttering talk about the judgments of high courts, and that the bail was higher than ever, and Jeffery who was higher than the bail. Who then stepped out wearing a straight tie and brown shoes and a button collar. His face was so pale they thought he was dead. He was judged and sentenced to hang upon the cross right beside the holy man who was picking his nose. And Alfred came to me with his arms open and wanted me to take him to the beach house; he needed a rest. The sabertooth tiger was chasing him across the state; poor Alfred he was too old to be governor, while his mother was still trying to seduce the statesmen and the night watchmen of the cuckoo-clock factory. But Alfred was only a pawn to be shoved behind the bishop who was disguised as a TV screen to fool friends and wealthy voters.

The steamship line is on strike, because the invisible man has taken all the money and headed for South America. With his things stuffed in a bag, he ran for the Gulf coast, because he was in love with the Pullmans son who just came back from the temple of the holy ghost with his pants down. And I was still in Santa Paula brooding over a new lifestyle in the Himalayan mountains, besides my groin hurt from the beating I took from a sadistic cop. Wouldn't you know it? A loud fool speaking on how un-American I was because I didn't conform to his sick society, but still asking me to bend over and take a screw in the ass, for some political gain and mythical power game. A sub-society springs up and the existing one strikes a heavy blow and someone gets canned because they weren't off the street by ten. Believe in my idea or I'll beat you to death, with no mercy, and they ran when it finally came to them. A coin found in my pocket had a face on it, what was his name? Oh yes him! They told me lies, who was he really?

Unknown date 1971

*1971*

**STREET SCREAMS**

The street screams!
I know it, man; I've been there,
in smiles, and death.
I've seen them come and go,
with whiskey, wine, and beer
on their tongues,
on their souls,
drenched to the bone
in the pity that kills them so.
The old man across the way,
who pees on himself,
who walks like a limp rag,
coughs emphysema into your face,
and calls you honey, baby,
and then slobbers on your cheek.
His sick smile,
that he buys beer
for everyone on the block,
because he is a sucker,
and an easy take,
for phony friends
that licks his ass,
and call him dad, or uncle,
or grandpa,
to get a little more
into their fat little hands.
And greed, and junkies,
and every man on the block beats his wife
black and blue,
everyone is on welfare,
and stays drunk,
because they don't
have to look at one another that way.
The street,
like tattoos that don't go away,
just grows rancid with old ladies,
who shift from window to window
peeking at neighbors' fighting,
and gossip wild unheard shit,
that flows and flows,

or until she becomes pregnant
and tries to hide herself.
The street,
and everybody smells the same,
and everybody dies
on the same day,
because they are all together
inside the old man's house.

May 27 1971

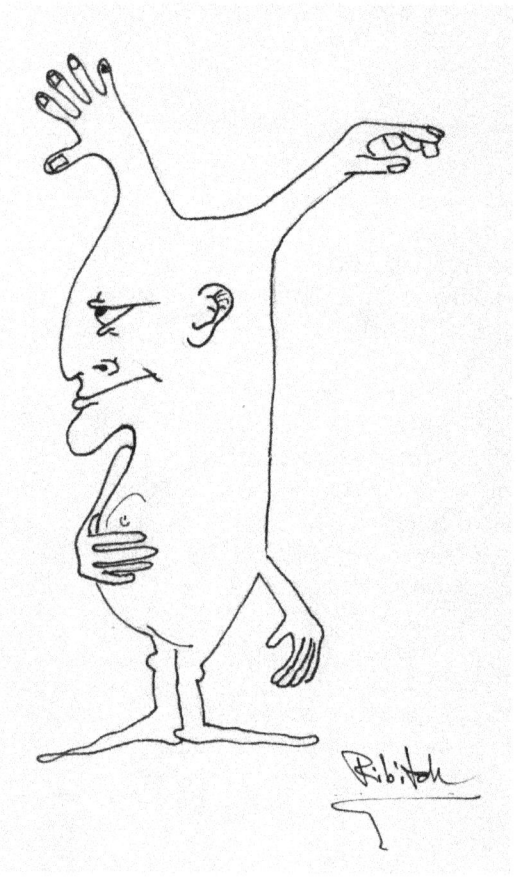

*1971*

**SUPERMAN'S DEATH**

We were part of that generation,
shot down by Superman's death.
Though they tried to fool us,
pushing on commix-book lies,
page after page, pushing on a steel giant
fake, a last push for pressing times.
But we remember you Superman,
the man of steel, and never ending grin.
They told me you committed suicide,
and I cried. But we are just part
of that generation that witnessed
the death of many of our heroes,
Howdy Doody, Hop-a-Long Cassidy,
not to mention the Mouseketeers,
now buried beneath celluloid graves.
All those visions of beautiful things,
and Superman couldn't hack the strain.
It was all on his back, but now it's on ours,
to die like the man of steel,
to be remembered in commix-book waste.
  Oh yes,
    Superman.
We remember you now.
  They murdered you,
    to murder us.

2/14/71

## THE BIG JOKE

It's just not funny anymore, the comedy, all the funky shit.
Laying down, another time the same related sequence, one number after another,
      1
          2
              3
Count down, again, and again.
There is no more time
    No.. .
        No...
            No...
Goddammit listen to me, the sickening humor is through.
Turn off the television set mind, recorded message bombs,
and exploding computer tongues.
    Stop! Now!
Because later the ends hang loose, and it just might sound useless and insane.
Turn on radios into the night air, fill it with ink blots and cartoon fantasies like screaming with your open mouth.
    TODAY!
Right this very moment, it's happened, and for Christ's sake, look at every body, just look...
    A fool's parade!
        A slime concrete desert!
Full pipes, trash heaps, and worries.
Endless rows of unsown corn, and millions, millions gone.
Now everybody's plastic Christ, and rubber Mickeys adorn their dashboards.
Don't call on God for protection; he's on vacation.
To lay away the monkey's paw, wishes and bad omens.
No more please,
    Justice?
        That makes me laugh.
Big deal, all that wisdom, and glory stored up for two-thousand years,
with a skinny man hanging from a cross yelling, "Father forgive them."
    "Father forgive them."
        "Father?"
           "Forgive?"
And they were forgiven, and they played more jokes, sat in more parlors, ate more food,
shot more shit, and cared a whole fucking lot less.

*1971*

For as it got bigger, and the bloated ego's rose, so fell under the working class hero.
He rode in on a pale horse wearing a white mask.
He was the superman of… Good?
    White mask!
        White Powered fingers!
What a goddamn rip off.
Let's tell more silly jokes, and lie to ourselves, it's not real anymore.
    So it's ok to turn away?
Ya! Sure, but the ends still hang loose and it still protrudes like a giant wound.
Screaming, giant soldiers run mad into hot fiery furnaces.
It's all on TV, at 11 o'clock, with Smiling Jack, bouncing on pillars of rain.
    Sure funny,
        Ha! Ha! Ha!
            In spaced warped history books.
Plenty of Ha Ha's there alright, between pages 137 to God knows when.
Still like the laughter and the comedy
    Red,
        White,
            and Blue,
                Stuffed shirt.
Alright, you dead ass wino, off your ass and pray,
    JESUS CHRIST,
A Holy Cinder leapt from the flame to blind your other good eye.
    TODAY!!!
        NOT TOMORROW!
Can't you see it, can't you feel it, and all that Karmic Sun bullshit…
Why are we dying, man?
Look, now beneath you are starving people, beneath you is your own image.
Right there, and all you have to do is…
    OPEN THOSE EYES!
        DON'T BE FOOLED!
Have the world, got silver dogs, to take on the game.
Civilization or the conquering hero.
    What was his name?
Glory, the blackened mouth that feeds upon the grasshopper people.
God heaves, the toothless, two-thousand year war.
A meeting of the people, throwing rocks and bottles.
Sitting in their engulfing machines, they pull the throttle.
The stars turned black… and time…?
Oh the clock, it has ended.

*Ribitch: The Last Word, Volume 1*

To all the words that are spoken, and all the people they offended.
       War machine!
             War machine!
Let me see your face.
I quit believing in the words that come and go from this place.

Unknown date 1971

*1971*

## TO BE YOUR CITY WHORE

To be your city whore,
In white bed sheets,
What is your claim?
That certain smile
That lures you out
To touch beyond
Your eyes,
To feel beyond
Your fingers.
Am I to be your mattress?
To collect the fees,
To please,
To be avoided,
But to be avoided.
A closet wall piece
To the rear of the mind.
What gentle respect
Is there from your touch?
Tell me I'm free,
But keep me
In the bondage of your mind,
Tell me of the pleasures
Of womanhood.
There can be no grapes
More bitter than yours.
But now the wind is changing,
All tomorrow
Is before me....


Unknown date 1971

## VARIOUS COMMENTS ON 4TH OF JULY

Ooo Ah, Ooo Ah,
Ooo Ah, Ooo!
    I like that one. Ooo Ah, Ooo
Ah, Ooo Ah, Ooo!
    That one was nice. Ooo Ah,
Ooo Ah, Ooo Ah, Ooo!
    Too bad.
Ooo Ah, Ooo Ah,
Ooo Ah, Ooo!
    My (clap, clap)
    My (clap, clap)
    The best yet.
Ooo Ah, Ooo,
    Is that all?
    BULLSHIT!

7/4/1971

*1971*

## WAR DEAD OR THE BAD JOKE

It's just not funny anymore,
the comedy,
all the funky shit
laying down
another time
the same related sequence,
one number after another
5
 4
  3
   2
    1
Count down,
again, and again.
No more time
No...
No...
No...
Goddamn it
listen to me!
The sickening humor is through.
Turn off the television set mind,
recorded message bombs,
exploding computer tongues.
STOP!
NOW!
Because later the ends hang loose,
and it just might sound useless and insane.
Turn on radios into night air,
fill commercial ink blots,
cartoon fantasies
like screaming
open mouths.
TODAY!
Right this very moment,
it's happened,
and for Christ's sake,

look at everybody,
just look...
a fool's parade,
a slimed concrete
desert,
full pipes,
trash heaps,
Worries,
Worries.
Endless rows
of unsown corn,
and millions, millions gone.
And everybody's
plastic Christ,
and rubber Mickeys,
for protection,
to lay away
the monkey's paw.
Bad omens.
No more please.
Justice?
Big deal,
all that wisdom,
and glory
stored up
For 2,000 years
with a skinny man
hanging from a cross
yelling,
father forgive them,
father forgive them,
father
Forgive?
and they were forgiven,
and played more jokes,
sat in more parlors,
ate more food,
shot more shit,
and cared a whole

*1971*

fucking lot less.
For as it got bigger,
and the bloated ego rose,
so fell under
the working class hero.
In white mask
that superman of...
good?
White mask,
powered fingers.
What a goddamn rip-off.
Let's tell more silly jokes,
lie to ourselves,
it's not real anymore,
so it's ok to turn away?
Ya sure,
but the ends
still hang loose,
and it still protrudes
like a giant wound.
Screaming,
giant soldiers,
running mad
into a hot fiery furnace.
It's all on TV,
at 11 o'clock
with smiling jack,
bouncing
on pillars of rain.
Sure funny,
Ha!
In spaced warped
history books.
Plenty of Ha Has
They're alright,
between pages.
stillborn laughter,
and commixs
Red, white, and blue,

stuffed shirt.
ALL RIGHT YOU
DEAD ASS WINOS,
OFF YOUR ASS
AND PRAY,
JESUS CHRIST,
HOLY CINDER
leapt from the flame
to blind your one good eye.
TODAY!!!
Not tomorrow,
Can't you see it?
Can't you feel it?
and all that karmic
sun bullshit...
Why are we dying, man!
Look,
now beneath you
are starving people
beneath you
is your own image,
right there,
and all you have to do is
OPEN THOSE EYES,
don't be fooled,
don't let those
corny jokes become the
cold farts,
of yesterday's pollution...


2/4/1971

*1971*

## YOU GOT A FLAG MISTER?

You got a flag, mister?
Hidden beneath your waistcoat,
I can tell by the gleam in your eye,
and your all-American sweatshirt,
that proclaims up your war,
and up your ass,
with Francis Scott Key
Tattooed on your tongue,
with the Star Spangled Banner,
oh how the rag does wave,
through our nation's perilous plight.
You got a gun, mister?
Hidden beneath your handshake,
and your smile,
and your dead war heroes,
that you wish to protect,
with your obscene lush,
middle-American homes
that hide away sweet daughters,
That shot heroin,
And O.D. alone,
Because you and your wife,
Were too busy to care.
You got a Bill of Rights, mister?
Hidden with all the things
You don't believe,
Like your smile,
Your faith, and religion,
Like the Ten Commandments,
And liberty,
Or words that you lost,
Like truth, justice,
And equality,
Because your eyes are closed,
And your heart is gone,
Like the great American dream.


May 30 1971

1974

## DAY BREAK

At the break of day I wait to see the sun,
and when the sun rises, I smile in its warmth,
and when I speak to whatever it shines upon,
it becomes part of me.

The fragrant warmth of the sea, to touch candle wax winds,
Sighing and laughing, over fields nearby
Where mustard is growing, like yellow suns,
touching my eyelids softly.

Unknown date 1974

## DEATH WEDNESDAY

Death Wednesday, just above ashen brown dirt-covered city grounds dwells, as if molten machines, body twists and jerks spasmodically in death thoughts of alley blood. Greyhound's new look jumps at glassy eyes and knee-bent winos; junk-starved veterans, cold stares, ten cent shits, and a fifteen minute wait at gate four. Loading for Oceanside, San Clemente, Los Angeles, and all points north. Can't shit anyway, some bum-fuck sailor fell-out O.D. on Quaaludes, gagged on his insides, and slit his wrist on his National Defense Medal. But somebody wrote an epitaph for him on the graffiti strewn wall...

> *"Death is madness become a brick! This sailor came out of his mind, and puked the signs of his nation, hot dog mad, mustard screams, urging Jack-in-the-Box tacos, friendly light-up war toys, Shell gas, Wounded Knee, Safeway, hated war madness. He puked till all that was left was fear, and here in this bus toilet he has found his new womb!"*

Unknown date 1974

*1974*

**FIRE RING**

Fire rings,
butterfly screams,
wailing the dust of
Roman deaths,
that sit alone
in love seats,
that crumble,
       scream,
                wail,
                            die,
and masturbate in the wind.


Unknown date 1974


**HEAR THE LONESOME WHISTLE BLOW**

I heard the lonesome whistle blow, past the train at noon,
and all the generals riding beneath the boxcars, like bums.
It was sad, with all their wars held tight to their chests,
coated by the fears of jobless orphans.
I saw the train die beneath the sunset,
the last caboose trailing off the end.
I saw the mighty nation crumble to nothing,
after bragging with boastful pride about its power.
Power that was left behind on the tracks.
A whistle blew in the morning for all the generals
were laid to rest, beneath foreign soil.
Off to the side of the water tank. I saw the screaming eagle
lying frozen, its eyes fixed on the flag.
It was wrapped like a tourniquet about the neck of some headless uncle.
War screams, death dreams, and a patriotic salute,
while bent over vomiting the over taxes for war spending.
Nuclear power,
       Power!
       Power!
Til it's all over by the dawn's early light.


Unknown date 1974

## I TOUCH YOU BENEATH THE SHEETS

I touch you beneath the sheets,
and you turn and smile,
we linger a moment
staring into one another,
touching with our hearts.
Then with flowing smoothness
you reach to hold me in the night air.
And I return my arm to you,
and in sweat, and love
we become one with each other.
Holding tightly to each other,
we pass the night,
and wake to our eyes meeting
and again I will make love to you,
and the room turns, singing softly.


Unknown date 1974




## JAZZ

Fade in and out, sound spills,
sound vibrations,
      Coltrane in the wind,
      Allison in the movement of the waves,
      Miles Davis in the continuing universes of sand pebbles,
jazz in life sounds, screaming gull saxophones,
wave against rook vibrations,
wind against the soul bass heartbeat,
sound escaping to the crest of the sky,
and hurdling earthward, to touch the ears,
      sound...
      listen to the earth...


Unknown date 1974

*1974*

**LOVE POEM**

I love you, like diamonds
fresh upon the sea.
I walk with you over sunlight,
and smile over the moon.
      I love you.
I could say it a thousand times
in a row.
      I love you,
and to you I give my soul.
      I love you,
kiss me and heavens will open.
Hold me, and all the birds sing.
Be with me, and we shall conquer the earth,
with smile, song, and love,
      I love you.


Unknown date 1974



**LOVE**

I love,
and I am loved,
tenderness is also strength.
I love,
and I am loved.
I am not alone,
I am growing,
I love,
and I am loved,
we are the light
that guides through the fog,
we are loving embrace,
we love,
and we are loved.


Unknown date 1974

*Ribitch: The Last Word, Volume 1*

**MAIDENS**

Maiden's ember dust
like lakes of swan's blood
beneath the willow's sadness.
Caress the fingertips
That lace through shoes.
From the swallow's roost,
heaven's landscape, where screams
bleed them like dawn
yearning in the sleeveless
Moon.

Unknown date 1974

**PAIN**

I ease my ass over, and shove it through the window,
where that gentle stare, where glass is broken,
      I scream...
      I am at fault...
Dying beneath a frozen foot, I creak across the floor,
blinded by such powerful dreams.
I cannot conquer this fearing mind,
thrusting myself past the ancient blue lights,
where fog lingers and stretches its fingers to remote rogues.
A waltz that cannot be danced to,
a flower without color
or a smell that cannot reach the nose,
but it quivers there in the black darkness of my weeping mind.
I am the softness of butterfly wings and the coarseness of fear,
my legs are rubber and standing alone.
I grow dizzy and flee into the stone of sorrow, where blanketed by dreams,
I wander, lost and afraid.

Unknown date 1974

*1974*

**SEA BREEZE**

I love you, sea breeze wind,
I love your eyes,
I love the soft touch of sand,
beneath my feet,
and writing love letters
before the tide.
I love you beautiful sky,
and all your magical birds,
and kisses of the wind.
I love you, beautiful woman,
and all your feeling
that warms me in thought.
I love you,
how I love you,
always.


Unknown date 1974


**THE DAY THAT BIRD'S BURNED**

The day that birds burned, their flame-like legs
spread open to the wind.
The day that birds burned, they bleed off in the open,
and split their bellies on the open trams.
They split upon the tracks their electricity.
The day that birds burned, their faces mirrored flame,
and all the hope that they mired,
set upon the dust ash of their soft brains.
The day that birds burned, they called out to hope,
and hope fled them.
They stood wasted, in their cloth dreams,
aflame in their tongues.
The day that birds burned, they sang in chorus,
the blood songs of their wedding,
and feasted in the fated
remembrance of the swollen.


Unknown date 1974

## THE DEMENTED VOYAGE OF UNANSWERED QUESTIONS

Into decadence she stepped. She seemed as if she had stepped from out of the past, like a giant toad de-fleshing itself in the stale stiffness of the room. This magnet of grace strode through the room like an ancient elephant of madness, and her mouth bellowed claps of thunder. She grinned till her face grew tight and cracked the plasticized cheeks like a doll crushed beneath fly dust.

None of us could quite place her, for this area of the world was barren and usually only mackerel, sea herring, and an occasional madman would pass by, under the feet of the shapeless multitudes. We were the old and tired shiftless broods, the same as Mephistopheles kept in an eggshell. We were the words of Rimbaud, the contorted hallucinations of Lorca at the moment of his death and the soundless screams of visionary eclipse. Our fingers bled from the tips and we sucked them harmoniously, giving out sounds of squeals and humorless laughter.

If she had really been there, riding the tips of our tongues, full-saddled and spurred, we would have quivered at her approach, and her nonchalant way of rolling her eyes back in her head. After she had centered herself in the exact center of the room, the exact position of the pyramidal orifice, she announced with a voice that emerged from deep within her chest that she was a student of the surreal, and that we were the goblets of the absurd. Our faces lingered awhile in the haze of the afternoon as she spoke of a lasting doom beneath the pyramidal arch of the studio.

"A student of the surreal," she said, "A student of the eye unfolded into the dreams of passion lit upon the soil of Dali's "Metamorphosis of Narcissus". She wept a little when we told her that the goblet was for fools. She ran her hands sown her doughnut shaped sides, and asked for a little time, just enough to moisten the crack in the sky, and she stretched out her tongue, which inched its way across the floor toward us. What could we do, except put on the chamber music and start the dance? Merced danced with Alfonse, who danced with the mirror images of defused characters, and I danced with Toni, a Pan-Asian witch, who performed her art of magic by the rose tattooed above her right eye. Her brow was shaved and the rose danced, we danced, and she, the student of the surreal, made only lizard noises and circles in the dust with her tongue.

If not now, then never, and if never then... Merced ceased the music by eating the radio, and Toni spoke in tongues and asked a question, "What is your age, dear?"

"What?" the student replied beneath her garbling noises.

"Your age?" repeated Toni, "Your age, in numbers that represent your existence? And you had better be quick; images tend to fade when your stare into them too long."

"Thirty-six and my socks are eight days old", she said. "What does that have to do with anything?"

"Thirty-six," scoffed Merced, crossing the room to tie the last bits of string to the end of the bed. "That I might believe, if you could only remove your head." With that she reached up and quietly removed her head, revealing another slightly smaller head. And this too she removed to reveal yet another slightly smaller head, she continued to do this until she had a pea sized head resting on her broad shoulders, and perhaps a dozen or more heads about the floor all shouting in unison, "Thirty-six, Thirty-six, Thirty-six, Thirty-six, Thirty-six,"

We all changed seats; standing on the highway was the same as being under the mounds, and we began to see the past lamentations of iridescent shadows into the hole of her life. The past was a mesh of conveyances, leather straps, and giant de-fleshing toads, ageless points of conduction, deduction, conclusions, delusions, and plays of uncertain malfunction.

She had been young at an early age, rumored to have been born an infant. Her vanishings were not reminiscent of her existence in the womb, but from postnatal thumbing from unqualified doctors, and unregistered nurses. She was a rude child, a figment of her own obscurity; her father was a wanton doll, and her mother was a rubber hose. Her eyes glowed, and ripped the flesh of the past with unsettling reminiscence of yesterday's flowers, flowers long since gone to seed beneath the blistering tide of phantom romance. For years her feet moved in silence, and her eyes could no longer fix themselves to the security of normality. She cared no more for the relevance of age than we did, and Toni's question had after all had been an ambiguous one. But for the moment, time seemed slanted backward. We had to continuously pick thorns out of our eyes, and look at our own faces turned inside-out.

Alfonse attached himself to the curb where he did little obscene gestures with his fingers, at a tree that paid him no attention. Merced, Toni, the student, and I stood on top of the bus stop bench and waited to make the same gestures to the sick and gray pelicans passing by. For every third pelican, we would freeze ourselves like statues and crumble into pieces at the foot of the bench, and with the fourth it reassembled ourselves with no more grace than a legless tightrope walker. We frowned at ourselves, taking out our hearts and letting them bleed. Toni's heart was blue, while mine was transparent, and the student's heart was only an egg, an egg of a yellowish color. Alfonse and Merced tickled their hearts, and stuck keys into the key holes, opened their hearts and removed their wallets. Merced's wallet was crying. Merced reached deep into his pocket and pulled out a quarter and inserted it into the mouth of the crying wallet, which turned into an avocado sandwich. Seven blackbirds dawning seven golden saddles, each with a green rose mounted on the saddle horn, came and plucked the sandwich from Merced's hand, and carried it high into the air. When they reached a point in the sky directly above our heads, they took on the appearance of an eye bearing a tear. The tear fell, and grew. We found ourselves stranded on a boat, with none of us with experience or knowledge of sailing.

Toni pulled out her eye from beneath the rose, and gently laid it into the water. She spoke in a language that I had never heard her speak before. The eye became brown as it floated in the teardrop sea, the sea dried. Where the sea had been there was now a great space of desert. We walked through the desert, growing painful in the sun, when we came across a man walking with his dog. The man was rather tall, bearing a star on his forehead. The dog was large and wore an iron belt around its waist. We approached them silently on our toes. The student was the first to speak. "Where are you from?" she asked.

"Venus," replied the stranger.

"Venus," spoke the dog, smiling.

There was a glow around this stranger and his dog. He held up a two-sided mirror, and said, "On one side you shall see your birth, and on the other you shall see your death, and on both you shall see the age of coming." We were amazed by the dexterity in his fingers as he tied them into knots. The mirror glared at us first from one side, then from the other. He smiled as we peered into the past and the future at the same time. He laughed as we saw our birth and death in the same moment. Our images of infancy and senility were the same. He twirled the mirror between his agile fingers, and life sped before us like a carrousel gone mad in a carnival of dreams. The stranger held the mirror up against the sun and reflected the light into our eyes. We were blinded by its brilliance, and while blinded the strangers' mocking laughter rose to an unbearable volume. We stood there in the desert, whirling in the brilliance of the mirror. And the sand was up to our knees. The stranger reached into his robe and pulled out an hourglass, which he held next to the mirror. He held it so that the reflection of the hourglass fell upon us. We looked at one another, seeing the fragments of age making their way across our faces. Toni screamed, because her magic would no longer work. Alfonse beat at his face, wrinkling rapidly under the sun. The stranger removed the iron belt from his dog, who had already started to change. The dog grew a series of horns from its head, its tongue wrapped slowly about Merced's body, and lifted him off his feet.

The stranger lifted his robe to reveal himself, and we saw that his entire body was covered with living tattoos. "Gaze!" he shouted. "Gaze!" The tattoos were of people, men and women of all ages. They moved about on his body, crawling across his glistening muscles. "Gaze!" he shouted again, this time with laughter in his voice. "Gaze!" We watched the tattoos while he held the hourglass above his head. "The age of coming," he mocked. And we followed the landscapes and cities, and the people moving in them.

We knew that age meant no more than the cycle of our dreams before awaking, and that each morning brought on only another day of dreaming. But in that moment we were the images in somebody else's dream, and they were awakening. I saw the first image of a newly formed tattoo appearing above his right breast, and before I knew it she was gone; Toni's image appeared in that spot. Again I saw a new image forming, and Merced took its place. Alfonse was next, and then the student, all becoming tattoos upon his body. I felt a strange sensation come over me as I peered out from his body, and then he lowered his robe. As the darkness fell, all of the past dreams fled over me, the studio, the student of the surreal, Toni's magical rose, Merced and Alfonse were dancing under the moonlight. I heard an infant cry and realized that it was my own. The dream was just beginning.

I could hear only one thing above my infantile cry, which was the stranger singing, "The age of coming, upon this flesh landscape. The age of coming, upon this flesh landscape reflected from the mirrors held by dreamers and fools. The age of coming, is like the difference between birth and death. From the moment of childhood fantasy, to ageless senility, the age of coming, the moment of crossing the barrier of time. The age of coming will be like the sweating dreams of madness, and closed doors that are finally opened."

Unknown date 1974

**TRANQUIL FISH**

Waves caress tranquil fish,
unbuttoning the rows
of pebbled sand.
The white caps kiss,
lovers embrace
the wind holds lips
that move in and out
of stars.
The sounds of love
reaches its tongue
along the shore to lick
the feet of the lovers entwined.


Unknown date 1974




**WHITE ROSEBUDS**

I love you milky white rosebuds,
soft as moonbeams of misty green.
Love like glass, on thin threads,
swinging in the breeze,
care not to upset the wind,
for fear to break the dove's fragile wings.
Thing seems to grow,
and my face is touched by the wind,
and your smile,
and your touch,
and your love.


Unknown date 1974

*1974*

**WIND BREEZE**

Wind breeze, I talk to you.
Love wink, I follow you in smiles,
lift with you to the sun, lay with you
under morning sky.
Caressing you in dreams.
Smile at me, and I become the starlight.
Touch a glimpse of love and growing whole.
Tender speed of thoughts in creative glance,
growing like lovers' time.
Kiss and touch, tender dewdrops.
Lover's laughter, my hand searches
for yours, in finding it,
my heart is filled.


Unknown date 1974




**WINE**

I long to drink wine
with you in the night air,
to touch lips,
and caress the warmth
of loving embrace,
I love you, deeply,
lovingly,
and want to hold you, with care.


Unknown date 1974

*Ribitch: The Last Word, Volume 1*

**YOUR ARMS**

Your arms,
speak into mine
in starry night,
to hold the blossom
of new, and growing love.
We kiss away any tears,
and hold one another
pressing the sun
between our breast,
and happiness,
between our smiles.
I love you,
like the splendor of time,
and our feet
will say hello
to many blades of grass,
as our hearts say hello
to the moistness
of the dew.


Unknown date 1974

*1974*

## BACKDROP TO A CITY OF FLEAS

Somewhere from the back of the head flow the eyes of nothing in particular. The flowers of wandering and blackout hallucinations are worlds apart with surreal backdrops, and stage plays. Speaking words, plainly flaying my arms wildly in the air, doves turn into bats, and the skies turn green for frozen lips. I can walk to the harbor to see seagulls' flight; they are hovering over battleships, screaming the defiance to guns dripping blood in the sun. A black cloud crosses the sky, brooding in the wind. Days get shorter and end in focus with the eyes of dead kings. Like Michelangelo's Sistine Chapel, peeling dead paint and crossing itself to the adherence of language, language is spoken and written with tools of the revolution, beheading the political misfortunes and disgusted placemats, and open oranges.

My eyes are pens, writing language in words that mean nothing on the sidewalk or between the cracks, murdering the feet of passersby, touching their legs, seducing their thoughts, breaking the monotony of existence in wavering torment.

Mothers suckle babies in parks and fathers rampage through nations, suckling wars on mechanical rage war dust, covering peace dreams with more lies. Murder in the dark corners of cities screaming out, screaming out dimebags, screaming out lust, screaming out past screams, screaming out with honking horns, screaming out honky screams in the street, past the Plaza, past the San Diego Harbor, past the dormant dreams of schooners, 28-foot long cabin cruisers on rich La Jolla soil, where intelligence rusts on the grass of wealthy homes. I, like Alfred, am dying on the beach with a finger up my nose in search for the hidden truths that escaped the writing on the bathroom stalls. And I, like Alfred, died on the steps leading to the San Clemente home of a barbaric fool, trying to glimpse the ruined remains of a nation that paid for a bulletproof swimming pool, driveways, and a leather custom easychair. And I, like Alfred, was afraid of San Francisco, with its tall buildings, and mindless unreality, and the same as San Francisco, L.A. consolidated my fears and made me puke in the green-grey filth of city air. Into the wind I cried to the dying dogs and cats in humane society cages, and for all the men and women in city society cages, and to all those cages, to all those cages, cages, cages, cages.

Eyeballs staring into glassy caravans, deep bottomless ideas of the social readjustment of certain revolutionary types, caught in the barb wire fence of the nation's capital that is crumbling on the surrounding grass. Airedales are pissing behind fire hydrants, where fireman beat the owner, and policeman pull down his pants to expose him to passing old ladies, who giggle, staring past windows that display a variety of intrauterine devices, rubbers, plastic dildos, and broken mannequins, with faces that stare out, cursing the eyes that stare in from the holes in the sidewalk.

A famous director films the air to beat off the flies, and imagery shadows that swoon from the spaces in-between. Arms of priests separate from the bodies of their headless fanatics as they cross the street fingering their noses, their religion and eating the holy bread. Drinking holy water, they pass the word, the word which leaves the mouth like so much of the ether stale air.

The Press Club, like the Country Club, is filled with drunken slurs about past adventures beneath the whale's mouth. I scream and then lick at my wound, roll over and glance at the bare bottoms of oyster shells and bird shit.

I never lead a studious life; my studies came from the street that seemed to be the educator of something better then mothball knowledge of dead professors. Literature is nothing more than mere language, and language is the sound of voices, and voices are the rejection of the treadmill that never stops, and the treadmill is in the focus of a competitive nation, and the competing nation swells the ballots, and bursts. Words fill the air like gases, and filters into the scream of the street.

I never did think too much of the camel's breath or his spit-in-your-eye aptitude, nor for the academics that smart-ass you to death with their knowledge of the law, when friends sit in jail for shit reasons, and their intelligence tells you that those people aren't real, and neither are you, and their academic soul doesn't know shit from green apples anyway.

I have counted my toes maybe a hundred times today, closing myself in the matchless wonder that every time I come up with a different number. I often wonder about the sorry superficial faces that appear as mirror images, while walking down the street at mid-afternoon rush. I glance past the waste on the sidewalk, grin at the stoplights, and with surprise at the asphalt, sighing with the relief of the sun fading in crimson setting. My feet tire from underneath me at times and the green, chipped bench beckons me with utter surprise. I grin again at the clock that is turned backwards and the flesh hanging from its arms, with time a transparent, ominous objection of lounges flapping the swords of voices, over and over in the ears of donkeys, in the ears of running mad men with fat wallets, and in the ears of eagles that are sold fresh daily for eight dollars a pound in butcher shops and underwear stores. Elephant teas run down the street overflowing onto the sidewalk from out of the gutters and into the open churches, drowning all the people. I watch with a look of scorn, and for what it is worth, death moves swiftly, quietly, and it matters not at all, for all their names could have been omitted from the obituary columns.

1/29/74

*1974*

**OF WEARING SMILES**

Of wearing smiles,
I dream of ostriches,
buried in brown meal,
combing their hair with fish hooks,
and seemingly losing their feet.
Inside cracked leather boots,
they catheterize their tongues,
and beat their breaths with bullwhips.
In length, ribbons are tied off into knots,
where seagulls pass, licking the sand,
and drawing figures
with the tips of their wings.
Seekers levitate
the golden stone past blaspheme's sorrow.

8/15/74


**TOUCH OF MADNESS**

A crisscross in the wind,
the mild touch of madness,
that creases the lips of fondled dreams.
I lick the eyebrows of bed worms,
and draw the blinds on my death.
The wagon that carries my coffin
has broken wheels, and the froth
that flows from the driver's mouth
is silver under the moon.

8/15/74

## DISMEMBERED SALAMANDER

Dismembered salamander
stalking the flavor of its tongue,
Breath vapors cling to the sun
while walking single-file
through the rose garden of flesh.
Thorns puncture eyelids,
Their sadness betokens
the veil of Rosarita's
death bed.


8/26/74


## SAND DOLLARS

ancient sand dollars
retreat to the look of eyes,
staring intently to the glass moon,
where the belief is…
a glass of wine in my hand,
and a seat on the next flight,
zipper chains swim
in my song with leaves leveled
at my chest.


8/26/74

*1974*

## WEARING THE MASK OF LORCA

Wearing the mask of Lorca, groaning lips, raw, peeled, and skewered,
hovering above Spanish landscape, in a death mask, a clever disguise.
Beneath olive trees, shot by Civil Guard, two bullets against the wall,
execution of a poet's brain, tearing the ripples of tears,
lifting tongue's delight, and swallowing droplets of blood.
Wearing the mask of Lorca, death twisted with eyes
lifting the sunset above Fuente Vaqueros,
where gypsies moaned, under the Spanish moon.
Wearing the mask of Lorca,
Federico García Lorca, I weep in your palms,
my tear ducts exploding dreams of flamenco guitars,
and tongues swollen, tacked to holy crosses.
Lips quiver the rage of pointless sorrow, beneath Spanish villas.
Ripe screams touch the night of wearing the mask of Lorca,
bedeviled and shot, beneath the Spanish moon.
Enriched the ripeness of roses, flowing red the blood of Lorca's face.
Screaming the midnight sorrow, with castanets singing to the stars.
His body is not wrapped in silks, and linens from Madrid,
but rough burlap soaked with the fever blood, dying of love.
He was squashed beneath the fields of poppies, a torso of regret.
He was dissected by the flies of yearning.
Wearing the mask of Lorca,
threading the needle through the eye of the poet's bleeding.
There is no escaping lips hurried by the bile of flesh,
sucking the minutes from clocks and fingering the petals of flowers.
Romance still lights the dungeons, where wearing the mask of Lorca,
is luminescent under the Spanish moon.

8/26/74

## AVIDA'S TEARS ARE SILVER

Fires thicken the execution
of serpentine tongues, and unhinge
the robberies of cerebral caress.
While days spent
underneath the razor blade
grins, with plastic teeth.
Dogs with two heads
moan with Franciscan witches,
who pick flies from their ears
to bead them into necklaces.
They adorn them
on their gowns of dream.
Tongues search for frogs,
where only images
of Dalí could be found,
and Avida Dollars
weeps but silver tears.

8/30/74

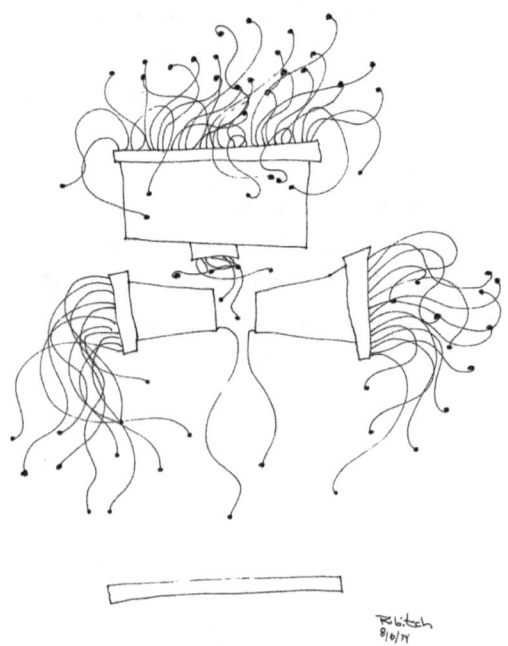

*1974*

## PLATINUM SCAFFOLDS

Stepping upon platinum scaffolds,
minted faces, and doubt,
rubbing foreheads sighing,
bleeding to death beneath
the fall moon,
crescent balloons exploding,
like faces of dust staring
at scarlet pillows,
where rainbows are bleeding,
where ostriches are dying,
where doors are left open,
where truths are invisible,
where canaries sing voiceless,
where graveyards hover,
where lips long for lips,
where love sprouts wings,
where eyes reveal tears,
where tears create rivers,
where rivers create oceans.


8/30/74



## RAZOR

razor blades
split the wrist of dolls,
thinking nothing but the wind,
i dust the table
of the crumbs of bread,
and seal the envelope
of sad farewells,
and break the plastic pencil,
while seeking out
the razor's sharp remark


8/30/74

## TOMORROW

Tomorrow when the sun rises,
the moon will still hover,
blue in the clouds,
and tears that wash away
the indigo crescent fill the street,
washing over the pebbles,
and the smiles of the past.

8/30/74

## BLADE SKIES

Razor blade skies,
fondle the blue of dying embers
that touches upon the wrist,
like satin bows.
My death
screams at my life,
and my life
weeps at its shadow
that lingers on an empty corner
where passes only the wind
and the sale of night jasmine.
The poster that has split its throat
upon the drinking glass
is filled with tears,
robins and orioles
that laughs at the disgusting
suicide on the floor.

9/2/74

*1974*

**LIPS MOVE**

Lips move, their entangled touch
caressing each spot
of tender romance
upon silver drums
and gleaming laughter.
We hovered in the night,
and felt the wrinkles of the sheets.
Love flies like hawks,
high above faces that linger
under the indigo moon,
gliding graceful feeling
of smooth silk,
and warm rays of sun.

9/2/74

## WEEPING

I weep into your palms,
and wear your love
where it touches my heart.

I caress the feeling
of your smile,
and touch your hand,
to vibrate joy.

I love you deeply,
as the tips of my fingers
hail out creations
that emerge from deep in my soul.

I watch you cross the room,
and let my eyes
kiss at your neck.

I feel your presence
and prow in our dreams.

9/2/74

*1974*

**FOUNTAINS OF SILVER**

Cascading in fountains of silver,
Savade slits his throat on a coke bottle,
and under his milky tears,
the flames of envy rode,
a steed that ran headless
into the open jaws
of remorseful vigor.
The goblet was stripped
of its silver plating,
and flung high into the air,
where oceans interceded
its valorous victim.
From the floor bled a silver touch,
the fountain was dry,
and left no love to conceive.


9/4/74


**HOLDING SADNESS**

I hold sadness in my hand,
like the three bubbles
and try not to squeeze too hard,
so as not to disturb their fragile grace.
Where eyes lift to see,
roses grow on the palms of hands,
and love's enchantment
sings out to ears.
They bow to their glacial counterpart,
so that lips will part
in the least amount of agony.
Love's caress must flow
with the sea.


9/4/74

## WAX FACES

Wax faces cracked into the sigh
of the candle's sad relief.
Tombs are broken into by mermaids,
bathing in motor oil, and sweat,
like the glass ships
exploding dreams into faces,
that emerge from toothless realties.
The moon with crescent smile,
bleeds upon open Eldorado's,
and saints and the starry-eyed clowns,
who in benign presence
vomit surrealities, and finger
their promises, like art nouveau doilies.

Wax faces that seem melted
from the hot baking in the sun
turn inward, with their lips parted,
and their eyes that seek out hunger
explore the satin dresses,
of manikins, cracked, yellow and dying,
bleeding, in the nest of ambiguity.

Wax faces, with senile breath,
tongues that stretch out
of third story windows,
on balconies of surprised sorrow
and relieve the tears of broken radios,
singing rhapsodies to the silent walls.

9/4/74

*1974*

**A DREAM OF PIPES**

A dream of pipes,
silver, gray, protruding from a wall.
Seven of them in a row.
What was an owl hoot
soon becomes a soprano note,
and ears listen intently
to the whispers of the moon.
A dream of dogs,
baying outside a window
that is lit up,
and which contains a face,
the smooth lines of woman's face,
hidden beneath a veil.
A dream of fire,
growing from my head,
and whispers that hug my chest,
and whales that swim in my toilet,
like planets in the constellation.
A dream of dreaming,
of being swallowed by a bird,
that sings no tune that
I can remember.


9/16/74

## A WAX MUSTACHE CAN'T TELL YOU A THING

A wax mustache can't tell you a thing,
it just lays collecting dust,
and waits for the wheels to appear.
It speaks absurdities to telephone poles,
and melts unspeakable laziness,
but you can talk to the pavement,
on cold rainy afternoons,
and hear the street whisper
long, untold secret messages.
A wax mustache just greases the space,
where words don't seem to want to linger.
A wax mustache can't be heard.
A wax mustache can't tell you a thing.

9/16/74


## POEM

Paste a dragonfly upon the wall,
touch its forehead with holy water,
and see if it changes
into a water faucet.
Glance to your right,
ponder what's happening on the left,
and dig a hole to put it into.
Slice an orange,
read to it poems from
Eluard, Desnos, and Lorca,
paint it with fingernail polish.
Stretch your face like elastic,
peel off the phony eyebrows,
and paste them
to the back of your hand,
and then call up the time,
to find out where to go.

9/16/74

*1974*

## PUTTING TOGETHER THE SPACE

putting together the space,
the empty draw at the top,
folding the leaves of a book,
so as to resemble a dream,
to become a marble footnote,
a statue in the corner,
with no feet,
the eye that is glass,
that resembles a marble,
the fragrant hint of musk,
the singer with no song,
the floor is cracked,
and all that lives underneath,
sniffs the dust like cocaine,
and eyes water,
and lips bleed,
and voices linger against the wall.

9/16/74

## WONDER IN THE POOL

wonder in the pool,
the freshness of beauty,
leaps from a lizard's eye,
and pounces upon
the hands of backward clocks,
suffocating the dagger-less heart,
mirrors beat the soft reflections
of unfamiliar faces,
and dance to the rhapsodies
of unfamiliar tunes.
where lovers entwine their thoughts,
and grasp with piano fingers,
at the velvet painting
of a rose in grief,
the moon makes love to its shadow,
on the moaning beaches,
under the searching tongues,
the pulse of a heart whispers
fleeting multitudes,
for all the ears to hear.


9/16/74


## MOMENT OF DREAM

the moment of dream
stretches across the forehead
to reach the lips,
with the utterance
of wildest imagination,
tippling the tongue
of tomorrow's sorrow,
and fingers the delightful
hallucination where the eyes
look under the lids.


10/17/74

*1974*

## PEEK BENEATH MY DREAM

I step from the end of my bed, and lift the pillow to peek beneath my dream, where swallows linger, licking the fog from eyelids, and dancing to the honeymoon. Songs that are sung from lips that have no remembrance, of nights that tasted like wine, and mandolins that weep fine Franciscan melodies to the soft caress of hallucinated dream, where fingers walk, to touch the touch of the midnight lagoons, and Aspen snows, cloud the frozen darkness of lovers entwining, where the pillow ends, and the midnight sea begins.

10/17/74


## TO THE WHALE

The decayed wind presses its breath
against the sun, vomiting the silver reflections
of monolithic dinosaurs.

Dying feet that peel their toes,
and nail them on the black honey,
they scream into megaphones,
where polite and gracious birds take to the wing.

Up thirty-six stories, where bankers record their death,
and ticker tape machines hum melodies of forgetful animosity,
and tearful nuns balance themselves on strung beads,
worrying about forgetting their vespers.

They remember the dying whales,
that have defleshed themselves on the avenue, in shop windows,
and linger long on flagpoles, eyeless, but remembered.
Remembered, yes, remembered off the coast of San Diego,
screaming defiance to warships, and slipping their blood
along the shore, where bathers weep in the sand.

The whales' dying epitaph, is written with their bones,
bleached, and cracked under the sun protrude from the sea,
and cry tears of salt and fear.
To them, with their mighty tails slapping the air,
I weep, for my mouth cannot form the words goodbye.

10/17/74

*Ribitch: The Last Word, Volume 1*

**WHAT HAPPENED?**

What happened
to the California pelican,
whose eggs grow soft on the rocks,
whose eyes fill with tears,
who dies beneath the oil-spilt beaches,
and weeps no more,
with mercury-filled fish,
bleeding on the shoreline,
where death claims the magnificent bird,
and histories are written
with invisible ink,
so that no one shall witness
their disappearance,
except for the eggs that rot in the sun,
and remain as monuments
to a poisoned world.


10/17/74



**SILVER FISH**

The gray silver fish that crawl amongst the used linen.
Break the spoons and spears, slit their throats on matchbook covers,
spilling blood, soiling the sky with red ink, and thumbprints.
Landscapes of towels are set aflame, where whole closets scream.
Below the touch of hangers hanging on lips that are parted,
with teeth gripped to the sheets,
and tomorrow spoils the mold collected in dim closet madness.


10/22/74

*1974*

## THE SPIKE ON INTIMATE SORROW

A seed hotly touches the eye, crisscrossing cerebellum dream, where naked roaches linger, condemning the dead. A horse's head disconnects itself, and weeps into the hands of priests, who dress like killer whales. They walk backward, counting their thumbs, and licking the armpits of the insane, letting the rosebud smile rip their lips, and decay their tongues. There is no hot relief, there is no neat white cocaine dust, there are no pale whaling ships, stabbing electric spears into blue rivers, erasing indignant relief, and rose's sad weeping hits the vein, where tattooed skulls remember all their dying songs.

10/22/74

## A DREAM

>Fleecing the wind,
>a cock crows,
>with a smile on backward,
>lips twisted,
>an inside-out remark.
>The sun rises in the south,
>conquering worms,
>delightful and splendid image.
>I talked to the back
>of my ears,
>and collected rubber stamps.
>Toes dig trenches in the sand,
>where eyes linger,
>and fat tongues
>talk limericks
>to wax mannequins.
>What used to be my feet,
>show themselves as bulls,
>entering hidden doors,
>with rat-breath,
>and a respect
>for the twilight hour.

10/23/74

## AT BREAKFAST WITH DRAGON FLIES

at breakfast with dragonflies,
aging spoons' laughter subsides,
where waterfalls end
in invisible rage,
a spoken sonnet forever tonguing
the white dust under the cover
of old volumes of Walt Whitman,
and his smile
that twisted up the gate
like a snake,
like the worn-out breezes,
that blow over landscapes
to the horizon,
scratching toes,
mingling with the crazed finger,
pointing in the air,
swallowing each bite
at breakfast with dragonflies.

10/23/74

## FISHING FOR A DREAM

A million sparkling smiles
that hover in the night
seek out eyes that linger
under the moon,
with cats moan walking
fever lash and breath,
aging mules become
themselves,
wanting to try their luck,
fishing for a dream.

10/23/74

*1974*

**NIGHT**

I stick toy fingers into the pudding of the air,
and whisper with fingers' tips to the frail cotton clouds,
that tick with silver tongues, the black phosphorous night.
With diamond eyes searching, from horizon to horizon,
I wield my sword, piercing the flesh of the sky,
and deflating the bulb within.

I carry a conquering worm, where whistling pigeons sing,
where high wires die, where robot angles turn around,
facing the pales of their hands, lifting their robes,
revealing scared bellies, and fingerprints painting
the lush outlines of tomorrow, where my face lingers,
with the song of the night.

10/25/74

**I FOUND MYSELF BLEEDING**

Bleeding in the basement,
with a dagger,
slaying eyes.
Soul filled and weeping,
an alligator crossing
the rivers that bleed.
Snowbirds metamorphosed
into faces licking the sun,
and a cockroach feels the scream,
that conquers mile-long memories,
that vomits the faces of ancient pelicans,
that grows old in their lust,
harmony, and spotless tongues.

10/26/74

## I SWALLOWED A JEEP

In distrust I vomit the rosebud smile.
Eagles that pose as generals' flag ships that piss in the wind,
and daring screams die, where old tombstones talk to thumbs.
Hovering over Asian landscapes, I swallowed a jeep.
With a toothpick in my hand, I pierce the tongue
of a thousand lizards, all talking to the cement,
I talk to the dust that is a brick of shit lusting its smell to the wind.
I cast a rose into the fire, and crisp my eyelashes.
A warthog crosses itself with the Madonna of light.
The soft bleeding hand and the tongue that itches,
means a whale dissects the wind, pursuing the spear of Ahab,
        and his leg of wood,
                and his heart of ash,
                        and his vision of white.
His vision of white was his vision of ivory,
and his vision of radio dust, where sick birds vomit.
To silk worm's delight a wooden stake is driven through his heart.
His vision is a Portrait of an old man eating an apple.
He was splitting the worm and vomiting the universe, while burning the toast.
I swallowed a jeep, a four-wheel drive that was bleeding, screaming, and dying.
Soaring above black clouds, singing, I am piercing with my sword, the gutless duck,
who only knows its name by the patch on the inside.
The walrus swallows my pride while eating a pigeon.
He spits in my face, licking my torment and then only sighing.
A dog lingers against the hydrant,
        hoping...
                What is his lust?
                    What is his true face?
His face that sees the legendary suck, that feels the proclamation, that contacts the blood,
that siphons the life, which is a lizard's bleeding.
An umbrella opens, spilling words, and ears that hear them.
A train enters a tunnel, screaming like a dead face that is my own.
That is my own, speaking a limerick about death, about life, about genesis,
about the hole in which the blackness spreads, and my love expels.

10/26/74

*1974*

## THE SONG SHALL END SOON

I pictured an eggshell exploding,
a windmill chasing the sun.
I wept, while laughing.
I saw the moon turn into ivory,
singing flame.
I grasp the dial on seeing,
and twist myself
into the knife of the sun,
and melt graciously
the blood of want,
where my eyes bleed
and torment the tortoise,
that only needs tomorrow.
A scream licks the dust,
and bellows the smile,
and dinosaurs stare out of streetlights.
Lifting sparrows on eyelids,
the dream I have is only a spark,
and I am throwing myself
into the mouth of the beast,
whose tongue is a jewel
of precious stone.
Is this a wax dummy I hold?
Is this my face?
      What?
      Are you sure?
Ok then, only your eyes will
see the dying sun.

10/26/74

## I AM A GIANT

I am a giant,
not seeing the sky.
I am a midget,
not seeing the earth.
What leaves fall from a tree?
What gentle angel kisses my head?
Tomorrow I will turn into a vase,
holding water or wine.
Tomorrow I will seek my feet,
and my feet will speak to me,
of places that I should go.
I will cry, and the tears
will fill my soul,
and rainbows weep sad farewells
to the rain.
I seek to touch my changing face,
to understand its intent,
to wonder at all the children's smiles,
and lick the honey of the moon.
I wish not to die wondering,
what is the bottom of my feet,
what is behind my eye,
what are the reasons of love?
I am a giant,
not seeing the sky,
I am a midget,
not seeing the earth.

10/31/74

*1974*

**I WANT**

I want to see a pirate flying,
where the sun kisses silver fingers.
I want to hold the rainbow,
and let birds fly without weeping.
I want trees to grow between the spaces
in the universe,
lick golden honey from eyelids,
break open a walnut,
and let fly the soft breezes
that carry the jasmine's breath.
I want to sing songs,
that nobody has heard,
filling the spaces with laughter,
tucking the sun beneath my heart.

10/31/74

## POSSESSION

The grin tied to a string,
speaks uneasy response,
where a spirit sat on his chest,
and tried to choke his soul.
But what of the scream felt inside?
But what feeling,
of fright and victim,
lays open the chest,
to steal the heart,
and fingers the mind
of uneasy grins?
To speak words,
that fail to linger,
that fail to touch the air
that crosses itself
in eager torment,
shaking in fear
where only clowns weep
on the opened chest
of running crazy.

11/17/74

*1974*

**SOFT BLOOD**

    I cremate the wind with my face that pretends it's the sun. A thousand eyes look into the throat of the fish, extracting my fingers that whirl like razor blades, and sink into the sky, cutting the clouds, and bleeding the sun. Such a fragrant mist that conquers the flesh that eats wholemeal cookies and that bleeds soft blood upon the earth.

    An apple, seedless, waxes my eye to see the sterile stomach swallowing my tongue. I am a seed of an orange looking backward into a room that contains only a chair, a picture on the wall, and a hole in the floor. I am a lip, cracked and bleeding, soft blood, rubber blood, soaking my flight. I am a bird, wingless, without feathers, without soul, that lingers long on antennas, speaking to the sun that bleeds, soft blood, wandering empty, out of shape and leaking, soft blood.

    Iron teeth, a will to seek into the wax face that meets me in the mirror. A withered smile, each knowing its own, bleeding its own, like the dust that gathers on an empty rose. I bleed, soft blood, and want to bite the sky with rubber teeth, lick the sun with asbestos tongue. What is this? Choking on a frail chicken bone and bleeding at the throat, I call out with soft blood, soft blood, always soft blood, that licks my eyes, and speaks of soft blood.

11/2/74

## A PART OF HER SUICIDE

An end to a moment, the last seeing of innocent rage,
where last twinkles the swollen dust of tomorrow,
where old dinosaurs die, clutching the spear of the wind.
To be born in the swallow dusk of spring, with each grasp
at what is life?

What is walking backward
        toward a dissenting day?

What is seeing inside your hand?
        And I smile, and love...

Birds sip the wine on the bones of dead whales,
remembered only as rosebud, the honky tonk queen.
She is licking her fingers in the soft night,
where the moment dies, lingering with the moon.
In pale moon, I lifted a glass of the soft-spoken executions
of stoic dream.
Scream the magnificent starfish lasting a single night
on a naked beach, sucking the black of night.
We wail soft melodies on a barstool,
And cry no melodies to the dying wind.

Picking ears erupting and vomiting in a glass jar.
What cross enigma rises above bottled sorrow?
where life rushes against the beast of fictitious memories,
and stoic imagination licks your hand, and swallows your smile.

11/21/74

*1974*

**A MAGNIFICENT BIRD**

a magnificent bird
flies backward,
into the eye of fools,
that cross the river's delight,
counting on their fingers,
rosebuds,
and smiles,
wiping frail the sky,
with vicious swipes
of the tongue,
and rose garden vomit
screaming the lullaby,
of jaded tomorrow
underneath flesh eyes
stare holes of fish blood,
and tomorrow scans
the far endings
of radiant dreams.


11/22/74

## AND WHO...

"A wax one," she said,
 crossing the room,
 stretching her fingers,
 bleeding the walls,
 with thumbs that have eyes.

"Bull face," was the other remark,
 one with the naked ape,
 the other with the slight
 smile lingering mood.

"I caught a camel pissing,"
 said the old crow,
 licking the sun's crotch,
 fingering the lips,
 between the legs of silence.

"And who said that?"
 was the whisper,
 that came from the hall,
 where only naked buzzards
 hidden in closets cry.


11/22/74

*1974*

**DIMINISHING MOMENT**

The candle diminishes
below the horizon, and licks
the eye of fossils,
a dead reminder
where the old fish swim
in pools of despair,
in skies of blue indigo,
in the rapid mouth
of lame dogs,
sung to the soft cobwebs,
that hangs upon the face
of old delights,
of new horizons,
and counting the lips
of migrant dolls,
that walk with the sun,
feel with the wind,
who speaks blasphemies
to the soil.


11/22/74

**OLD MOVIE**

I end my face on a flattened plaster wall,
where donkeys migrate and a caller door
squeezes its lips into rage.
The solar eclipse of a wandering face,
smiles above rich laughter and doors shut.
Windows break, the soft breakfast breath.
What cattle walk among strong air?
They ask for directions south,
speaking in Latin tongues to rebel nuns,
holding fish hooks in scaly hands.
Rose bush eyelids push back the blank
stare into tomorrow's stomach, where old scenes,
from old Bogie movies unreal themselves
on dusty theater floors.
Pools that haven't been swum in
in two hundred years, of old movie propaganda,
filter the dead dreams of legless track runners,
fleeing from tall buzzards, in Lincoln Continental smiles.
Legs that are cracked stand to the formless
vision on avenues, where streetlights bless the naked babies,
who dressed in sunglasses, eat all the manhole covers,
and make remarks in the fever of blood
and in the distraction of blind wonderment.
Pools of sight, form the rails beside
tanks of rubber cement, that held the city together,
and a solid dream, speakers stand above velveteen platforms,
sculpting the dawn on the horizon.


11/22/74

*1974*

**TO ME**

Bring me the wings
of a breakfast soup,
toss me the sight
of longitude romance.
Kingly discretions
fondle them
in lunch baskets.
I am waiting for my reward,
golden earrings,
with lips singing
a soft mood,
and a gleaming sky,
unfolding the dark past.
Birds that strip feathers,
and bath in melon syrup,
talk to me of sweet wine.
Caress my short,
and tangled beard,
lift my eyes
to soft dream
lamp light,
and squeeze
my angelic body.

11/22/74

## THE DEMENTED DOG

The hand rose above silver clouds and gray matter caressing the skyline, where soft minds vomit in the streets and where plastic saviors deflate the body of the holy perfect and Christ sips a malted, behind sunglasses. Crying dogs swear upon the cement soil, and lick the stone asses of eager police, running in place with paper feet, in water buckets. The rose-colored faces are embarrassed and perplexed, where magic bleeds, where stone houses sit alone always in broken chairs and in broken chains with broken hearts.

Bleed silver dogs, bleed as you weep. Conquer the sapless trees' eager flaunt of decadent surprise. Who knows what fragile superman breaks down to weep on fresh flowers and to stagnate the wind, breaking up the formation of stars? Stars that blink with no surprise. It will bleed open wounds from the sky to earth, from head to foot.

Pant on gray lame dogs, where your feet are swallowed by cracks in the earth. Breathe hot breath to the fires of lingering souls that haunt Dante's swollen eyes. The gray of the brain stretches the sky over mounting sky towers, lifting windows where fingers touch the frail velvet of crazy weeping sighs.

When does tomorrow touch you, chrome dog? Who licks your waxen tongue? Break me like a twig, fevered dog, and dance to the bleeding moon, underneath the jasmine's silk gown. Play with legs of forgetful sorrow, needling the soft-spoken memories that entwine the turtle's' eyes. Blanket the steam, shove the curtain open and smile sweet memory, where aproned asbestos dogs claw the agile face where sympathetic rubber hoses beat black and blue, the swollen cheeks of deserted dancers. Ribbon trails the gut, up the chest, to waiting lips that savor the seed of rotten fruit.

What kings have been dethroned, in past centuries that were leveled with the axe? Token coins hang around the throat, where the slice of meat bleeds and hungry dogs wait in earnest hunger, with their tongues pierced by their own teeth. Their eyes are glued in backward. A swallow's roost is torn down in fright, where fear strokes the two headed coin and eats lunch after dark with morticians and widows who dress naked. They cut their wrists with razor blades and peer through veils with sad, softened eyes that wail under the tender touch of blackened tomorrows. Now see it sitting with laughing demented dogs that choke on bones and die in the fevered sun.

11/23/74

*1974*

**I SEE CINDERS**

I see cinders,
burning the cities,
where the cities
should have been burned,
banks crumble,
and bankers
whimper in the dust,
streetlamps flicker,
shops have no shoppers,
fur shops have no furs,
there are no animals
the air is thick,
the sea is dead,
and I see cinders,
burning the cities.

11/24/74

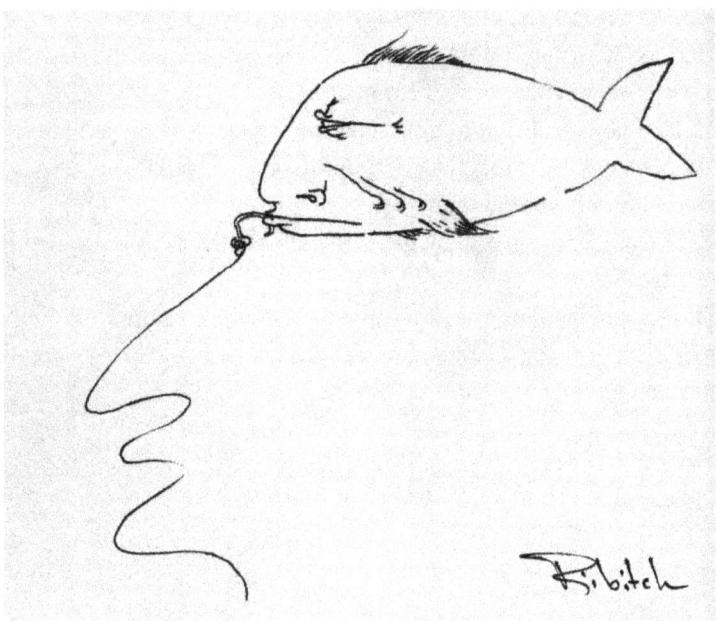

## SEE WHAT GREAT EXPECTATIONS

See what great expectations, in the rose,
held in the hand of Rimbaud, who wrote in a letter,
>   *"The poet is the thief of fire."*
Then truly to be the thief of fire, beyond any night,
to steal the lips that live beyond the tumbling wastelands,
beyond crystal horizons and beneath the point of the pen
that etches such timeless energies, far beyond any boundaries.
Men who are fools think that such things are a waste,
and that the product is not nearly worth all that,
That which can be folded in billfolds.
Their brains are obsessed with the pleasures of material delights.
But who speaks for the poet, who works in the foundry,
turning the lath, and tending the shop, when fingers search
for a more meaningful existence that touches the entire realm
of living, and scratches the surface of eternity.
Then truly to be the thief of fire, where madness rides a wild horse,
to reach into the far corners of my mind, to leave no pain
or joy untouched, and wields my pen, my sword,
to cut the gashes in time, and lift the soft melodies of the heart.
This is where poets sing them by the sea.
I am a poet, and I lift myself upon the platforms of my madness,
where my fingers touch the gift of my dreams, and linger,
with the soft mirrors of my pen.
The tears that I shed, shall give strength, to my art and meaning to my page.
If my soul is eaten by hungry giants, and only a single word remains,
I still shall have stolen the fire and placed the flame in my cup,
and drank the pure warmth of the sun.


11/24/74

*1974*

**I SEE THE BONES**

I see the bones
of old dinosaurs
walking naked in the swamp.
Cobwebs bleed,
on their backs.
What fiery breath
they did expose,
past the swallow's dawn,
where the past
is quartered
in a rummage sale?
An old box makes
stale the old loaves,
and the dying
embers of tomorrow's lust
lie across
a dinosaur's tongue
that speaks no
tomorrows
that I can hear.


12/3/74

## THE FROG'S KINGFISHER

The frog's kingfisher,
doubles up the knife,
switched to the heart,
screams the veil
over the dead,
knotty pine box,
eagle prints,
sail heavenward,
on a green bicycle,
lips speak robots,
valley of sand,
today's tomorrow,
fills fish bowls,
with silver water
and glass lips,
fly in the breeze,
where moments
collide with the dawn.

12/4/74

*1974*

**BLOWFISH**

what blowfish
screams across the bay,
with a smile,
and dagger,
to stab the hand,
rubber, pink,
black and blue,
with a finger
of a rose,
that sticks,
the air,
with warble smiles,
lifting a beard,
for all to play,
and all to sing,
and all to lift,
the bird on the wing,
sticking two Siamese
cats in a dime.

12/8/74

## WORD PLAY

Look at the plastic tongue,
swiveling above ground,
with eyelashes,
and glory,
atop a skyscraper,
with middle finger,
of latter day
raspberry pudding,
who plays with words,
three dot syllables,
in three row sequence,
with nothing to spare,
but loose change,
and a Davy Crocket
hat from Disneyland,
and lost in the shuffle,
a card named
the ace of dukes.

12/18/74

*1974*

**VICTORY**

A rubber zipper flogs the inside,
of the madness of the emperor's face,
eating a donut,
licking up the chocolate syrup,
from the floor,
where ants linger,
speaking of old cartoons,
and they migrate with fresh glances,
to spiral eagle,
and two-tone dogs,
with lots of chrome,
battle breath,
laced with the shoe,
forgotten... forgotten,
legs diamond,
in his tea suit,
machine gunning,
the mad grins,
and speechless victories.

12/31/74

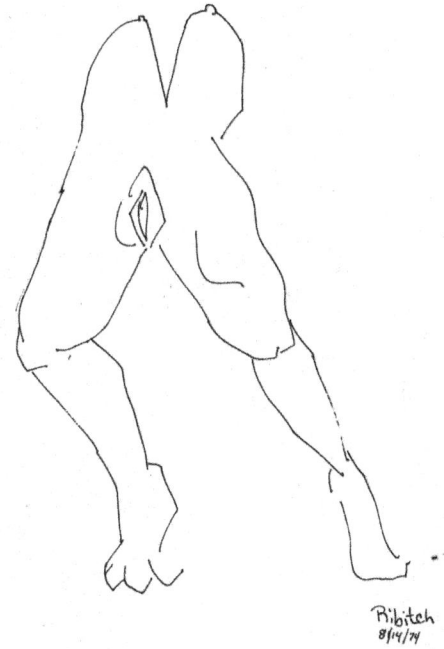

1975

*Ribitch: The Last Word, Volume 1*

## PHRASES COMPILED (for Malcolm de Chazal)

What hungry vermilions swallow the tigers tongue, lust as parades end, or in flag relief and fog chances of leopards whistling at the moon,
      1/3/75

Imagistic relief of the soul of my symbols, like the crest of a rose it is revealing uncertain truths.
      2/3/75

Who would kings be atop loafs of bread, stealing the hungry sugar of wailing tears that resemble rose petals in the eyes of watchful energies.
      3/1/75

Who would be kings atop loaves of bread stealing the hungry sugar wailing the tears that resemble rose petals in the eyes of watchful energies?
      3/24/75

To flee the city on granted wings and herring bone saddles while the tortoise flame eats with hungry spittle and the flower of the night.
      3/24/75

Saturday's full of shattered moons and a small naked bush leading to and fro in the dust of an ageless past,

songs of the day exploding, exploding summer's death.
      2/12/75

Time reads nothing in empty space, words conquer all dreams, and lift the space above the universe.
3/1/75

A possible conclusion of a fact, a total realization of a moment, in a house made of fog, invisible, but solid, transparent but all seeing.
      4/1/75

I see the sea of marching fingers, lapping at the cold mist above the sand, holding itself in blinding white foam and licking the thunder underneath pebbles, where ancient and glorious dinosaurs play till the dawn.
      6/1/75

A possible conclusion of a fact a total realization of a moment in a house of fog invisible but solid

transparent but all seeing
      6/11/75

While writing something for my tombstone, I used chalk and the rain came washing it all away.
      6/11/75

I looked into the mirror, it shattered and carried away my face.
      10/3/75

**1975**

What brings this year to an end?
The eating of a nation,
the starving of a people,
a cold fart in the wind that signifies
the dying of presidential powers.
Who puts blood in your pillow?
Who speaks in tongues?
Wrap the year-end in frayed linens.
Questions asked...
Where blood dies like leaves.
Where the year died with the nation.
When the nation frees
the culprit with stained pardons.
Jobs lost...
        Jails raped...
With justice fingers
twisted around the neck of liberty
who slits her wrist while watching satellite TV
Moscow burns in Los Angeles
with Sixth Street bums who didn't catch the last act,
when Caesar was thrown from the window
clutching his nation in his pants.
Where despair feeds on the hungry
and the Golden State is buried in shit.
The wings fell off a bird, an eagle I suppose.
What strange illusion extracts a coin bleeding?
Who wears the crown of a dying moment?
Licking the sun, turning in the foul sky
a crooked finger pointing to the multitudes.
Crying, their hands are pierced
with the midnight sorrow.
Crucified to the high-rises and the temples of cash receipts.
What brings this year to an end?
My tongue stapled to the floor
with the endless news commentary
giving historical reports and other obituaries.

1/1/75

## THE ROAD BY THE SEA

Whisper to your blacksmith,
intone the road where rocks fill with
the moon's hovering cherry,
and dogs lay down by the sea,
sinking into spasmodic smiles.
Do you not remember when
the lost smiles lasted so long
and the greaseless night
broke the boat away
where cinders burn the sea?
A flight of ducks flew
into flames wearing no
asbestos suit, or guile disguise.

Eyes cannot clutch eyes
in depth hovering of blades.
A taxi warped and screw less
is a bowling ball sighing?

Lake of the tide,
of the completely senile rose,
of the postage stamp war
and lengthy fingers
rubber stamped against the sun
burning in small flesh sequence
the tar pools tear
at the sight of four broken jailers
roasting the goat at dawn.


1/3/75

*1975*

## I LICK THE BLADE

I lick the blade
that slit my face
that still hovered
in the gray distance.
What stale desert
defeats my feet
and hungers my soul
when pigeons eat my eyes
sidewalk passions suck dry
the empty shoes
of clay feet.
A cry in the wilderness
in stocking feet obliges
the soft wet under bellies
of inter-woven apologies.
The air stands empty
and my tongue touches the map
where roads end.
with the scar on the moon.
A day without green shutters
flying in the breeze
and no expectant crowd
to linger on any avenue
with no utterances of
dead poets that plead
with undertakers
or under water faucets
speaking French to walls.

1/6/75

## LIZARD SKIN ROSE PETALS

The window on the frozen dawn,
past the sparrows' spiel
with tongues of elastic
and swords of vapor tears.
A river running silent
bleeding with finger tips
laced, another shoe
full of shotgun shells.
Eyes of eagle shit
possessed the demon soul
of flowers pressed
and grinning.
The day ends in dust,
the radiant cover of
the sun
that vomits again,
again, and again
while shedding lizard's skin
to rose petals.

1/6/75

*1975*

## WINDOW ON THE FROZEN DAWN

The window on the frozen dawn,
past the sparrows' spiel,
with tongues of elastic
and swords of vapor tears.
A river running silent
bleeding with finger tips
is laced, like the other shoe
falling from a shotgun shell.
Eyes of eagle shit
possessed the demon soul
of flowers pressed
and grinning.
The day ends in dust
And the radiant hover of
the sun that vomits again,
again, and again
while shedding lizard's skin
to rose petals.

1/6/75

## SENILE DOGS ROAM

Senile dogs roam
through some aimless valley
tugging at worn sleeves
and cutting the ties
that strangles the tongues
of voices no longer
reminiscent of the fevered smile.

Laughter rings the triumphant
burst of its swallowed halls
and stains the floors.
No face lingers against the clock
no switchblade eyes
cuts the stomach of gods.

The lake has lizards
polishing chrome.
Naked eyes peel
off noses and rub
their tongues in ash
puncturing their eyes
with salt,
but this worm bleeds,
where no stone
speaks at ill.


1/9/75

*1975*

**FLOWERING DOGS**

Flowering dogs
peddle eyes to look over,
the ridge at your face,
and the symbolic tongue
that stretches across the face
of time,
of one foot,
of nine minds,
      gone,
      gone,
to the true silver dollar
encrusted into the palm,
like an electric knife.
Cut the ribbon
of your smile,
touch of the spear,
that tacks
your soul to the ground.
Wax the false doll,
whose image is
a T.V. test pattern,
frosted to the
glass pane,
sucking the last
breathe laughing.


1/24/75

## THE MAGNET OF GRACE

Whose pale body
is crossing mine in dust?
The magnet begs at my heart,
loving the only fragrant flower
that touches my soul, and even then,
        I cry,
        I weep,
        I touch the mirror
                of my face.

Lips eyeing the afternoon
and all the birds leaning into the wind,
are touching their laps, hailing their laughter.
What frail humming bird
licks the flower's crotch,
and receives the bliss
of tomorrow's romance?


1/24/75



## LOVE POEM I

I lift into the spectral horizon,
and touch my eyelids
with the foam of the sea.
I love in the sky,
like birds,
like soft wind pillows.
The starry night
blessed mood,
and rainbows,
to touch my face,
to touch your face,
smile like the sun.


1/26/75

*1975*

## MY BRAIN PLANE

I stepped from my brain plane,
and goosed the dream,
with a pin, and a feather,
only to see the darkened umbrella
give wings, and take leave
of sanity's rush.
Pick off the hallucinated dragonflies,
ask their tongues
if they need to leave,
in sorrow,
in respect,
in a Buick,
painted with no paint.
It's a fleeing zebra,
no face,
yet talking,
yet flying on no wings.


1/26/75

## WHO FETTERED INTO THE NIGHT

Who fettered into the night,
past blind street signs,
speaking to the dust,
living in the wind?
Whose days last fade into the smile,
when days bleed,
and crosses into the spaces
of the air?
A wax pear
enjoyed by my tongue,
lifts a parade,
with bands of seeing-eye tubas.
A score of weightless
astronauts hover,
swallowing birds,
and playing chess,
with no eyes.
With no eyes,
every doughnut shop
on Hawthorne Blvd. is stripped naked,
glazed and baked.
All that is rubber stamped,
sees the whole bird
stepping from a flag,
and dropping dead
and falling from a coin.


1/26/75

*1975*

## A MANNEQUIN EATING FLESH APPLES

A mannequin passes out
in the back seat of my car.
It was dead I believe.
The cold of the flesh
ate at my hand,
that ate back at the flesh.
The mannequin lusted
across the seat eating apples,
and passed out in ray car.
The engine was dead.
As dead as the mannequin's face.
No total eclipse of the moon
evades the lost brain child
who walks naked and alone.
the mannequin stares
at the soles of feet
lingering beside the frosted well.
The mannequin feeds lust,
touches the only heart
that bleeds upon the seat.
It eats flesh apples
upon the open roof,
vomiting the steering wheel,
eating the sun,
stretching across the face
of leered dolls
who speak mannequin language
to the stale air.


1/29/75

## HAND GRENADE

Hand grenade,
my face is lined with cement,
no quicksilver,
or mercury pools,
deadened fish speak,
no holes in ray hand.
Hand grenade,
touch me with moss
of dead cows,
let linger the prayers
of mosaic platforms,
cut off the necks
of monolithic seekers,
who stone themselves
along the shores of dead rivers,
a bird slips
into the foam of night,
and eyes all the victories
of frozen generals.
Hand grenade,
don't follow me past the pit,
or eat at egress,
and no rocks to touch
the leveled space
in the empty drawer.
Hand grenade,
no rose wilts
under your gun.

1/29/75

*1975*

## I SLIP OUT OF MY SLEEP

I slip out of my sleep,
and piss out my window,
on birds passing by,
who only mock
with stale laughter
at fragrant winds
that blow over dusty horizons,
executing television sets,
and shopping backwards
threw old stores,
with old and dying
dinosaurs in heat,
but who believes
in the unholy wind,
and its cross
that bears initials
across the sky,
where dogs linger
under the moon.


1/29/75

## NO PLASTIC GODS

No plastic gods
are put asunder,
leaving behind the foot prints
of dying warriors,
who earn their tongues
with flaming dollars.

Ask what bird
dies, leaving its feathers
to dry along the shore,
where beagles press
their face with chalk,
and burnt wooden crosses.

Tack the face to the wall,
vomit the eyes of leaping dogs,
who are senile and lame,
but who conducts
a symphony of strange delight.

Who bleeds from heaven,
slicing their wounds,
and touching their faces
with feathers,
and cut glass?


1/29/75

*1975*

**WEREWOLF**

Eat the night, swallowing the moon, naked on the branch.
cry into the space of empty eyes, and seek to hide
beneath the belly, torn open, and bleeding.
Padded feet touch the stillness, guiding hunger
past swollen eyes, and nailed to the post.

Moan in the closet, beneath torn coats pleading with fear.
Into mirror faces that are changing needles' flesh,
eating roses of the dead, and stealing faces.
Playing on the mind, what no gypsy can play on the guitar,
The song of fear that is blood red, and speaks to the moon.
They all walk backward, stretching their laughter along the wind.
Streets die, saving only the soft mood of savored blood,
that lingers only with the aging tombs of forgotten worms.

So lamplight wanders, wanting to kiss the soft dead lips
of angry devils, that threads needles, and pierce the flesh of frozen dreams.
Wax memories drip are leaving no scared under bellies,
to soften the evening's wandering kiss.
Dawn bleeds the hand, with fleeing claw, and death waits
the sun on the garden, where the roses plead with the thorns.

1/30/75


**CAMEL**

Did you see the camel, humming in the wind, with a wax smile, changing his bed clothes that were soiled? His lips are backward and bruised, his face copying the face on a coin, but broken like a glass. There is only an eye to look across the alley, no windows to peer through, no satin flesh to stroke, or beacon rubber stamps to veil the rose, on the lamp, and the camel refreshes the smile of the desert's warmth.

2/2/75

## POET ASSASSINATED

    Peering up from the bathroom floor, eyes glazed and dead, murdered for a word, no less a thought. He had hungered from those lips, an ancient enemy and was stoned and quartered. His soul fleeing from death's hand, sought to rest beneath a root, crying past no junk hunger, a need to be heard, to be found, not in fame, but running wild, screaming to the world it's only face, that refused to look back into the eye's, of the stone dead.

2/2/75

## FRESH CLOVER

Standing under the fresh clover,
with a revolver, a skillet and a face.
Stretching the sky in my fingertips,
I knead the yellow ball of the sun.
My mouth is full of tongue.
My words form fresh langue,
and I sail outward with my hand
to touch it lightly, like it was a feather.

2/3/75

## TENDER DEVILS

Who speaks to tender devils
that linger in the solitude holes
that fingers the mind?
Let me speak to them,
let my words run crazy,
like the fires in the wind,
and speak to radios of the past,
that only wanders with
the soulful spies
of my want.

2/5/75

*1975*

**THUMBELINA'S DEAD**

Thumbelina's dead,
and I cried salt tears,
because she used to
dance above my pillow,
and wink soft surprise,
under the laughter of the moon.
Dreams flow from
the pillow's romance,
and lovers crossover
each, other,
blinding the sweet memory
of their embrace.
But Thumbelina's dead,
screaming in her death,
her rage,
that touches my face,
and scars my heart.
Who pulled from my pocket,
a reed and a childhood,
that never grew from my pestilent past,
like a growing laughter,
that caresses the wind,
and becomes soft beneath
the pillows of my dream.

2/5/75

## THE FACE ON THE DESERT

She stands alone in the hallway. Her breast is sewn together with threads. Her eyelids filled with lead. The blessedness of her soul vanquished in the desert dust. The moon is of honey, vomiting at her feet. In the stillness she sings with the radio, and fingers the rose imprisoned within iron gates. The bird in the cage is dead, wilting its beak and holding onto a ribbon. Its eyes were holding a vision, and its claws holding its heart. No one can touch her face because it is bleeding. Yet her smile is invisible along with her touch. Though her tongue is pierced with needles, she calls out to the wind. "Let me falter under your gaze, and perhaps shiver under your touch. For while I am lingering alone with this death, the rigor mortis passes from its body into mine."

The bird whispers from the bottom of its domain, he can't whistle, and you can't run. Your legs have been sawed off, and my beak holds this ribbon. So while we both lay motionless in our death, let us dream of toothless realities that bite at our eyelids, so that we can't see the floods that gather at our feet."

She walks legless holding the cage, and whispers wordless infinities in the desert air. "You know well my delusions," she sighed.

"Yes," replied the bird. "They linger on my eyelids like a cancer and finger me with pointed remorse. My madness is yours, like my tongue that tastes the night,"

She glanced downward sadly, only touching her teeth. What had seemed clear was always a puzzle, and the vacant memories of her youth caught up in the maze of walls that surrounded her. She bled there, looking across the sands. All the hallways are not far behind. "What is your eye, is my heart," she said," to the bird. "…As sure as I have been hung by this ribbon. We are seekers, and our eyes have been plucked by the scrotums of our time. The ancient dinosaurs die at our feet. We are missiles in the air. Expending lives as our deaths, beneath the willows of our tears."

She held up the cage in one hand, and a piece of mirror in the other, so as the reflection caught both her face and the dead bird. "Let me take your ribbon," she said. "And tie it around my hair, or at least let me steal your wings and fly away from here."

"There is no flight," said the bird. "That is an anonymous request. Even if I were freed from this cage, I cannot conquer all of the bondages that have blinded me."

"There is stillness in the air, and it touches me with fear," she remarked.

"A stillness that rocks with the force of a hurricane." hummed the bird, picking up on the music of the words. "It fills the whole of this desert, and chokes the sky."

The desert air was hot and still. Only the stars gave hint to any life in the sky. She half delivered herself here. What began as a dream, and the dream had touched her eyelids, and frosted over her soul. She was awake.

## 1975

Her dream was her journey, and her journey was like the sand, a forever kind of thing that stretched from horizon to horizon. "Did Lawrence really love the desert," she asked.

"Lawrence was a fool," replied the bird. "Not to mention a butcher."

"But did he have a purpose?" she asked.

"His only purpose was his desert war," said the bird. "Yours like mine, to find and shatter our mirrors. To bury the knives that slit our throats. To seek endlessly our freedoms, and to wilt graciously beneath the flame of our needs,"

The desert sand burnt the souls of her feet, and roasted her eyes till all she could see was the red of her anger. "Fire!" she screamed. "Mixed with my blood, and stirred with my tongue." She sat down on the; sand and wept. Crystal tears touched her cheek and froze.

"See," said the bird, "tears are hard and can cut your soul. But all the same they can soften the wind and lift the flower on your thoughts."

2/15/75

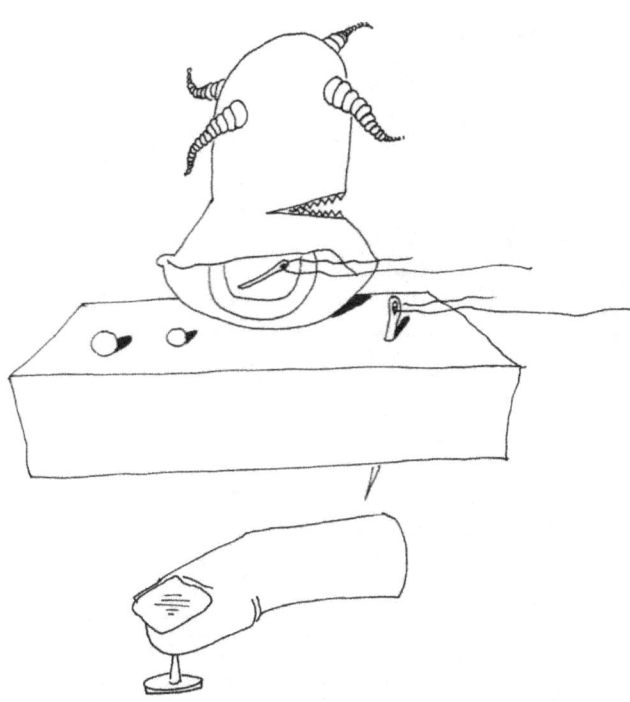

## THE POET'S CALL

I step off the end of my words,
where my pen ends, and laugh
at the wind.

I can talk to the unseen,
and bathe in written language.
What forms a word that
caresses the mind?

I shall speak
some unwritten melodies,
and converse with the spaces
between the air.

The world explodes,
where fires dust their tears,
poets linger,
and fight with demons
of their time.


2/25/75

*1975*

## I TOUCH THE WIND

I touch the wind,
with my eyelids,
as the breeze passed my face
where I linger,
I sing with the night,
and hold myself erect
in the wind.

Where do I cross over
the boundaries
into my soul,
and touch the windfalls
of stormy screams?

I am a mirror on the sky,
fulfilling destinies,
as ripe as summer pears.

The sun's flagstone
ellipses the mired rubble,
and lets a hand of fingers
reach into the pocket
for nameless clocks,
whose hands clasp my hands
and dials the minutes,
breaking the time.


3/1/75

## MY NOSE IS STUFFED

My nose is stuffed with somebody's boot,
I breathe, through the mouth, to make my throat sore,
and my eyes burn, to lift my nose,
again above the clouds to smell the sun,
to smile naked in the breeze,
or in the chattering ceiling of the sky,
where birds gather to fly around the soft clouds.

3/1/75

## SPITFIRE

Spitfire above the eyelids,
where crossed third eyes
walk on in romance
under trees,
under the moon,
under the scream of night.
I love like the fires,
hot, floating,
flying in love
above fire's flame.
In love flying.

3/1/75

*1975*

**A FORMAL INTRODUCTION**

Meet Clarisse,
who touched the face of monkeys,
touching their palms.
On Flag Day she dressed
in the drapes of nations,
and quartered the moon
with nickels.

Meet Bonaparte Livingstone,
who ate at the luncheonette
with all his tongues,
and fat lips,
resembling mattresses.
On Independence Day
he drove himself insane,
and locked his brain away.

Meet Bonito Sonata,
who died in the lobby
of the Chase National Bank,
counting his coins,
His hands were all thumbs,
and silver burned them,
making him bleed,
and cry.

Meet Francis Tromain,
who beat herself with cheese,
leaving marks on her body,
and holes in her soul,
like the wires across
her face that dug
into her eyes,
leaving all the walls
crumbling.

Meet Amelia,
who threw away her keys,
after locking up the wine.
With no food in her belly,
she sang to the richness
of the dust-covered floor,

and bled with the rats,
who came naked,
and paraded across her forehead.

Meet Adeline Baker,
who broke her mirror,
when it came to close,
and twisted the pieces of glass,
and stuck them into her eyes,
where she could see
visions of the Armageddon,
where the beast
feasted on her feet.

Meet six,
who are joined together,
like Siamese twins,
linking their fates,
with their faces,
and traveling among
the stars toward
unseen destinations.

3/2/75

## COMPUTER DREAMS

I am standing in the foam, with what bone meal freshness
attached to my feet, like the arcane mumbling of leprous robots.
Computer dreams caress the feeling fingers that wait under the
hallowed moon.
Spacewalk in capsule of time, where energies erupted the tiny belle of
the wind.
A wax dream haunts the hallways about midnight, when eyes bleed in
the dust.

3/9/75

*1975*

## GIANT

A giant steps from behind a rock and squats, he produces a hundred birds, all with silver hair, and to each one, he slits a throat, and pulls out another bird with hair of gold, and to these he bites their heads, and reveals for each bird, a hungry dagger, resembling a key, that he unlocks the gates, and releases the chains of power madness, each with the look of a dragon, that eats its hands, and sits on the lonely rocks, piercing the sun with a simple hatred.

3/26/75

## SILVER BIRDS

Silver birds climb the ageless wind
and lick the sky like tomorrow,
a "blanket of wetness,"
sings melodies
to the cotton clouds,
and covers over the sands of now,
while still hovering, a song bird
sees all glass seas
speaking tongues to radios.

3/26/75

## I SAW MY MOTHER

I saw my mother,
standing naked amongst
a grove of trees,
she was no longer,
the tall slender, dark
beautiful woman, I had known,
but she had withered,
and grown pale.
Her hands were no longer
smooth, and agile,
but twisted, and swollen
of arthritic pain.
She called out to me,
"y mi hijo, mi nina,"
and her voice cracked ,
and faded into the air.
She held out her hand,
and in it she held
a heart pierced with an arrow.
It bled droplets
that fell at her feet,
where roses grew.
"I love you,"
she spoke to me,
but I did not listen,
because the words
had boxes around them,
and the boxes were of lead.
She reached inside of her chest,
And removed a photo album
Containing memories of our youth
They had stains on them,
her tears that she bled.
She showed me a picture

*1975*

of her and my father
embracing beside an old car
by the sea,
it burst into flames.
She showed me a picture
of my father and me smiling,
it turned into a bird,
and flew away.
She showed me a picture
of my sister, and grandmother,
sitting beside a trailer,
it fell, and exploded.
She showed me a picture
of her with a famous singer laughing,
it disappeared.
She showed me a picture
of myself in a high chair,
it turned into a bubble, and popped.
She then removed her face,
and folded it,
placed it into her purse,
and from the purse
she took a camera.
She took my picture,
and I disappeared.


3/27/75

*Ribitch: The Last Word, Volume 1*

**THE ANGEL OF TRAFFIC**

I saw an angel at an intersection, with wings of wood.
The angel was directing traffic.
The angel had no arms.
My eyes had turned to glass, and were frosted.
What whales had turned to gold, ripped the seams
of the Lady of Fatima's dress, and ran the angel over.
The angel's feet, that were nailed to the pavement,
remained revealing silver toes, pierced with rusty nails.
The angel sat beside the road.
The angel wept.
The angel arrested the reckless driver, and screamed a nightly prayer.
I took a cross, and placed it where the angel stood.
The cross was directing traffic.
The cross had no arms.

3/27/75

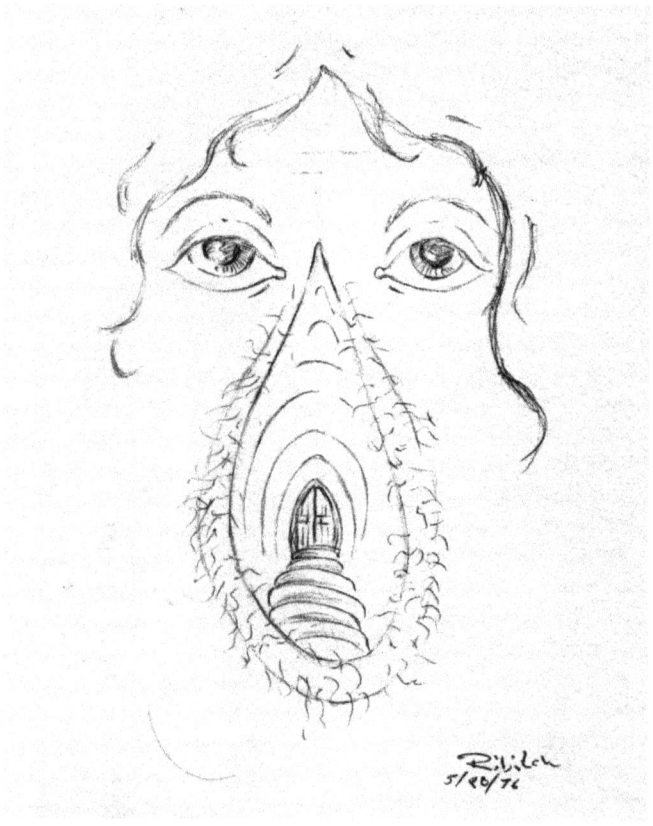

*1975*

**THE DANCE**

When the dance was over
they sold the bleachers,
carried off the windows,
and hung the band.
The music resembled
stale plaster.
The organ grinder smiled
at his coffin,
and drowned his monkey
in the French quarter.
But who savored
shoes of patent leather,
with taps on the heels & toes?
When it wasn't Valentino,
for his feet were buried
in cement,
of fameless sorrow,
and all his followers
tore down the shrine.
But the dance
was painted red,
by painters of the Rue Morgue,
who spoke only Latin
in the toilets,
and drove Chevys,
across the bay
to the widowed grandmothers,
weeping in the frothy dawn.


3/27/75

## WHO SPOKE OF THE WOLF

Who spoke of the wolf,
but his own grandmother?
who mirrored her madness
in a death squeezed
seconal smile?
She lingered on in hunger,
rich, but not famous.
Her ghost who was rib less
and spoke French
with an angry tongue,
while she rode through
New Mexico on
a new Harley Davidson hog.

Who spoke of the wolf,
but his own grandmother?
Though not very loud.
She whispered his name
in some death struggle,
choking the pain
of reality living,
and spit at him,
again, and again,
drowning him beneath
her death dream mad rave,
that then simmered the heat
of no laws remembered.

Who spoke of the wolf,
but his own grandmother?
who was physically beautiful,
but whose soul,
clutched the ugly madness
of her death dream.
She conquered no daily delights,
but fell to her face,
holding the last passion
to her gnarled breast,
a dollar bill, and a mirror,
that reflected her daughters
sorrowful cry
in the same death spasm dream.

*1975*

Who spoke of the wolf,
but his own grandmother?
Standing on her tomb,
retching out her pleading night.
She bled into a napkin,
and stuffed it into her mouth,
so her words were muffled,
beyond hearing,
and she sat high in her beauty,
admitting to no one
that she would no longer
speak of the wolf.

3/27/75

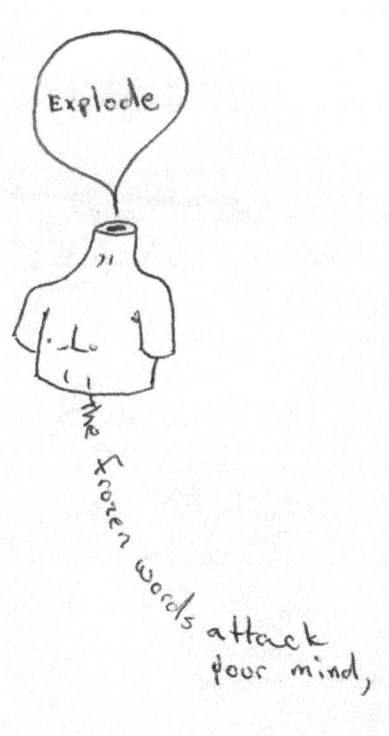

## ZORRO'S CHEST

Zorro was a bandit,
he stole my mother's liver.
He had a chest in which he kept silver coins.
He placed it inside the chest,
and he crossed Himself.

There was a rumor,
that he stole
and gave to the poor.
That was a lie.
He kept it all inside
of the chest,
and gave to nobody.
He stole my father's eyes.
He put them inside the chest,
then he crossed himself.

Zorro wore a mask,
so that his face could be hidden.
He had no face,
it had been placed
in the chest,
with my mother's liver,
and ay fathers eyes.

Zorro's horse use to have
great feet, until he secretly removed
them in the night.
He placed the horse's feet
into the chest,
along with my mother's liver,
my father's eyes,
and his own face.
He then crossed himself.

Zorro ate breakfast alone.
His mouth had been
sewn shut and crows sat
across from him,
the crows winked at him.
He snatched their beaks,
placed them inside the chest,

*1975*

and crossed himself.

Zorro was a mad man,
his mirror revealed it as truth.
He took the mirror,
placed in inside his chest,
along with my mother's liver,
my father's eyes,
his own face,
his horse's feet,
and the crows' beaks,
He then crossed himself.

Zorro had wanted to write
a letter to his grandfather,
who he long since placed inside
the chest.
He frowned at himself,
because he could not write.
He took his fingers,
placed them inside the chest,
with my mother's liver,
my father's eyes,
his own face,
his horse's great feet,
the crows' beaks,
his mirror revealing madness,
he no longer crossed himself.


3/27/75

## GLASS BIRDS

To many glass birds
vibrate themselves
into the whole regions.

Birds cry silver tears.
Flight with wings of lead.
Robot freshness,
smells of the rose,
of fragrant holiday of wind,
of decaying
in the mirror of romance.


3/28/75




## THE DWARF

The dwarf ate himself,
starting with his feet.
He canceled out his eyes,
and threw his arms
in the air,
where birds plucked them,
and flew away.
In his death torment
he fell out of his brains,
and broke his heart,
he now lives in the waste basket,
where no songs play.


4/1/75

*1975*

**I AM**

I am a face,
a mirror place,
a tune in the back of my head,
I speak of walking,
stand still, beating the wall with doubled fist.
      I am...
      and I will...
I roll inside of my brain,
like dice searching for number seven,
and coming up number nine.
      I bleed,
      I bleed,
I look inside my face,
though it is backward,
and the pieces lay within their grasp,
like a broken egg, bleeding in the dust.

4/4/75


**I HEAR EVERYBODY TALKING**

I hear everybody talking,
their words are plaster,
cracking, and dying,
      like so many times before.
What is there to say, but words?
      paint,
            images,
                  tongues,
that lick the air, and spoils the fragrant mist of tomorrow.

4/4/75

**I SAW LORCA**

Frozen beaches lay open,
where cities rest,
where cities die
from tormented suicides,
and the sand has changed
into blood prints,
of old faces
lingering in the haze
of a mountain screaming.

And I saw Lorca bleeding,
he was wearing
my face,
and he slit his wrist
with a sewing needle,
while saying his nightly prayer.

The painted suicide,
pleas with chamber's sorrow,
glistening the whole
of the face in the mirror.
A naked rose,
and a reflection,
a resemblance of tomorrow,
who sits like a mountain
with stone image.

And I saw Lorca,
severing his heart,
with a silver blade,
and that was his suicide complete.

4/4/75

*1975*

**ROOM OF BOLTED DOORS**

    I stepped into a room with bolted doors, where rooms resembled mirrored cities, flesh towers of fingers, and wrists protruding up from the sands, of eyes that are glued backward to walls and timeless clocks lift themselves above rich ashen laughter. The room bled in angry relief, revealing cold dust bellies of scared birds shaving the minute partials of the wind, with their upturned beaks. The water pipes come off the wall, and seal themselves to throats like weather vanes. The paint becomes dragons licking flesh waterfalls, and caressing the molded face of leopard's dance. The room breaks into its shadows, its blood-stained rafters, factories emerge from single cells, and convicts elude themselves by hanging their hooks with perforated ropes. Their necks snap backward, leaving no leather bathers to strip the sun of its scream, or backward melodies inside of speechless radios. Dragonflies eat themselves, their savored tongues lapping up their breath with their hands, and chains that wipe the lips of monolithic fish.

4/27/75

## FLOWERING MONOCLES

Flowering monocles
        dust
the rim of over conscious
        slipping,
                sliding,
past the avenues,
        and windows
of frozen dreams
        pipes
lead softener
        and old dogs,
                hungry at bay
At noon
        on the corner,
under the leaves of naked
mermaids, who in their laughter,
        of salt tears,
put them in boxes,
for all the dwarves to steal.


6/11/75


## FROM HERE TO THERE

Race across the universe, tagging all the spacious
fiends with your eyelashes, let them fall into your mouth,
like canyons deep, like flesh apples in the sun,
sun explosions, in the fevered heat.
Roasting the swallows' feet,
        ranging from here to there,
        ranging from here to there.
Flying like a rose, across the wind.
        Ranging from here to there.
A heartbeat bleeds itself, in traumatic chatter,
always wanting to bleed alone on the steps of a, hundred years.


6/11/75

*1975*

**SILENCE**

A lifting silence
        touches the end of your ear,
and helps itself
              out
of doors,
        that remains closed,
for a while,
        ears speak
out to tongues,
exchanging true glances
to the fog ribbons,
              and mist


6/11/75




**SPACE BETWEEN THE TEETH**

There Is a space between the teeth
of ancient bones and cracked oatmeal cookies.
automobiles, flatten themselves, on freeways,
to lick at the open wounds  with pointed tongues,
and slip down by the sea, to see the bird's flight.


6/11/75

**THE TOUR**

Couldn't see Europe
on the back of an ostrich
with fins and dual tail lights
       CUSTOMS
flies on wings
bleeding all the space
that jazz musicians
talk of in tales fevered robust of souls
fading into the French landscape.
The bird fell on its face feathering itself
alone under the boulevards


6/14/75

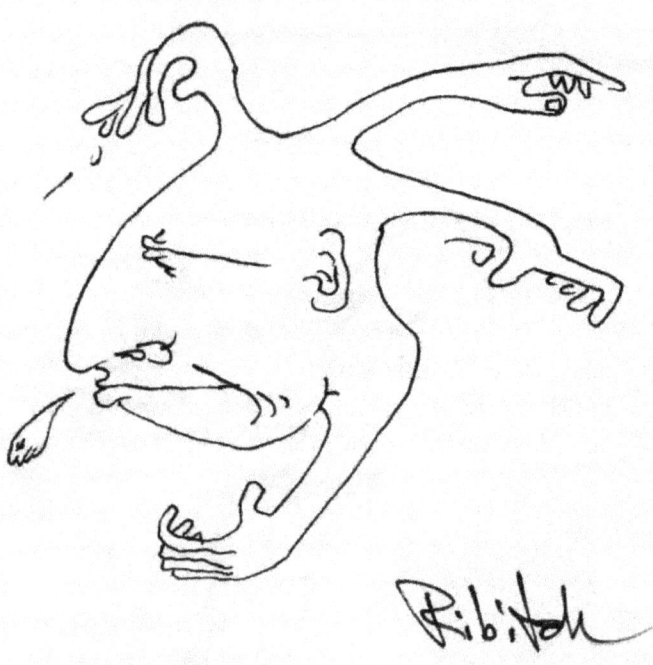

*1975*

## CAMEL MOON

Silver horses stride the blue dappling wings
on the yellow sun eating apples over the blue pudding sea.
Lover bliss, touch their hands in the velvet sky.
Tongues lick clouds resembling bears.
The sun is shining today and all of the lovers
call them out to bathe naked in the warmth.
Skin tingling freshness, ruddy cheeks, bosoms and bellies.
Fingers that close around fingers.
Lips that touch the fragrant blue dahlias laugh intently
amongst the wild greens and warm summer flavors.
Today love is shining with the sun, with the eagle's flight.
Winging graceful dances, feet leaping high
above the lovers' bed and camel seas.
All the light shatters prisms of rainbow kiss.
The dawn smells of clover wine and of dawn sweet
lovers moaning the richness of an embrace.
The sea fills with salt tears of joy, and holding erect
the flowers of dreams.
The pillow sets aflame the dance of the sun
where lover spenders the melodious madness morning,
of skin on skin whispers tinder the camel moon.


6/21/75

## LOVE POEM II

A wax flying
rosebud dreams
lick themselves
in the tender morning
under the fragrant dews
and listing lovers.
The spacious clocks
tick in the morning haze,
laugh in the morning sun
and fly in the fervent mist
of often dancing,
of often singing.
Seeing the dance
speak of rosebud rainbows
and the dew
hovering about the corner
of often speaking,
of often sliding off the grass
and into the break of day.


6/21/75

*1975*

**SUN**

I feel the day
blistering all the warmth
an the blissful array
of tomorrow,
of today,
singing songs of hollowed night.
Speak tender tongue,
speak of forgetful animosity
in the hallways
where gazebos catch fire,
where flame bleeds
into the night
swallowing the dream
repose of tender touch,
of days,
of wine and freedom.

6/21/75

**THE GOLDEN LEAVES**

The golden leaves
drop from the trees
bleeding past autumn
into summer
the glass eyes peer
into hallways
into the mind
into the whole sphere
of living
        NOW!

6/21/75

**ENERGY HORSES**

Energy horses
exercising the wind
with rose pillows
and wax breath.

The feathers of the sky
finds itself in the bleeding
moments of cosmic flash.

Bird doses
look at one another
with beak eyes
and crossed fingers
of diamond love.

7/14/75

THE coat tails
of the Rabbits tail
Quivers in the lost
horizons of
Concocted memory!

Ribitch
8/26/79

*1975*

**DANCE**

Who wants to listen to the wind
as it bellows yellow
above the cloud,
fragmenting the stagnant sun,
and sucking the foremost
energies of futile power.

No rose blossoms
grow in the garden.
No voice speaks
in tongues to the blowing blades,
that grip at toes
that linger too long in the haze.

Who wants to listen
to the poets moan?
Dancing in the warm
afternoon of a jelly sun.


7/17/75

## ATISCADEL

Atiscadel, the blue knight rider
with his horse of flame,
and his sword of ice.
Who bleeds the soft moon
sparkling day
where soft parades
eat the morning lunch?
Egg sandwiches divine.
Shallow peace.
Dime store lemonade
poured into reddened ears
and mouths open
to swallow the whole agonies
of Saint Francis,
nailed to a billboard
speaking restive suggestions
out past the harmonious leaves


7/19/75

*1975*

**BLUE FLAME**

glass birds streak the sky
like blue flame
living the white light
inside the eye
that travels
to inner perceptions
and fleeting
cosmic realities
in the haze
of blue flame
bird's wings
touch the tone of cheeks
asking for
the kiss of the sun
the whole earth rhythm
the bees sing
melodies to the sky
that burns the blue flame

7/19/75


**CLASSICAL CLEARING**

Must you seek the clear resin with your hat looking so? Your skin has fallen off, and is replaced with walnut shell. The fragrant mist caresses the whole wheat of your face. A man who calls himself the skinned wiener Oscar Meyer bow ties, yells in the split pea sky and swallows himself at your presence. do you speak to me tonight? Your tongue has a knot tied in it. It reminds me of a walrus in heat. "Oh you kid, you fool roasting the jellies of explosives in your house. What? Oh yes that|. That's what it's always been.

7/19/75

## LAUGHING ON THE SPECK OF DAY

The intelligent spiral napkin needs its tongue
to break the dust of breakfast laughter.
The sun is water eating fish, where the daylight
speaks to the brown stucco angels
who dress themselves in white linens
and roll themselves in cotton eyes.
Barren birds and eggless nests
of eagles laughing
at the pure points of dawn
laughing on the speck of day.


7/19/75




## MUST YOU SEEK THE CLEAR RAISIN WITH YOUR HAT LOOKING SO?

Must you seek the clear raisin with you hat looking so? Your skin has fallen off and is replaced with a walnut shell. The fragrant mist caresses the whole wheat of your face. A man who calls himself the skinned wiener Oscar Mayer Bovinetus, yells in the split pea sky and swallows himself at your presence. Do you speak to me tonight? Your tongue has a knot tied in it. It reminds me of a walrus in heat. Oh you kid! You're a fool roasting the jellies of explosives in your house. That? Oh yes that, that's what it's always been!


7/19/75

*1975*

**SIGNS ON THE HIGHWAY**

The rolling beast
thunderous breath
the beating wheels
of America's silent bird
white caped and bleeding
a sword entered
its belly
by way of its mouth
and vomited
the color ejaculation
folding in the haze of
morning disgust
white bread burns
on the highway
where ants gather
to sacrifice
the holy significance
of torn crust
and gather the ashes
to mold them
into statues of
famous T.V. dogs
who are split open
and lay like Burma Shave
signs on the highway


7/19/75

**BLACKBEARD**

Did you see Black Beard
as he sat atop
his flagship,
and counted skulls
of conquered flags?
And who bled
this weeping day
from the clouds,
like a sponge
touching all the madness
in the hearts of the sane,
like a rose-filtered dream?

Black Beard's only fool
sat alone
on the ship's toilet,
contemplating tiles,
and beating off
in calypso rhythm,
while the ship sank,
leaving the bleeding wood
to float in the sea,
collecting seagull shit,
and Blackbeard
who lost his breakfast,
over the side,
complained that his wealth
had followed.

3/27/75

*1975*

**NOISE**

To tell the truth.
        To tell... to...

Ahhhhh, Ahhhhhhhhh, Ahh, Ah, A...

There are four small turtles speaking,
They wear pill boxes in their heads.

0' hummmmmmmmmmmmmmmmmmmm

Black birds sing melodies from old Victrolas.
They know their own voices by the tires that squeal in the night.

            Clang  Bong

Who is going through the dresser?
Who is speaking from underneath the bed?

Zzzzzzzzzzzzzzzzzzzzzzzzzzzzzzing

Breakfast is at dawn.
Cornflakes bleed like wounded buffalo.
Captain Hornblower speaks.

            Putt-putt-pow
            Bang
            0' fizzzzzzzzzzzil, snap

When the sun goes down the wind breathes
When the wind flies
I count the days

            Buzzzzzzzzzzzzz

Ok, ok, ok, ok, ok,
The rebel yells in the dark.;

7/28/75

## SHOT GUN

Shot guns rang out beside my bed. In the hole illusions of dangling frightened dogs ran at bay singing to nuns who are birds roasting in the parade of dream and wetness. The loud barks of screams from barrels that harness the blue dolphin scream.

Wet night.<br>Tonight.

Bleed sorrow on wireless radios. Blankets bleeding the soft bird's heart and heat to play with words electrocuting the burnt wind. Flesh maniacs roll their tools. Crescent-wrench, hammer stains and rolled oats fed to monkeys who speak French without tongues. A blast from black tongues, in which the spiral hood of hounds crossing the street in a hurry, to avoid the crossing of crosses and burning the light and seeing the eye that stands at three feet.

What?

All those spaces fall into each other knowing that all of them carry no spare. Knives kiss the apartment of blissful rage. Where pelicans carry shot guns and shoulder belts. Eat the sea that turns orange under the bleeding wrist of flying angels. No memory apart from that which enables the swollen leopards to speak.

Can you top that? Can you bleed soulful and discreet?

But soul of shotgun desired parade lapses into the box like clouds that turn keys in the sky. The white smoke of birds leaves empty drawers on the yearning table of dreams. Foster's Polaroid sunglasses are on the inside of Ramal's blindness. As shotgun madness dream sees all the flesh tying knots into steel girders. No flashiness of blood fears the tears of the soft angels breath. The face of the earth dangles its blow before the latent dawn, and speaks words for the wind

"Shot gun, shot gun, shot gun, shot gun."

7/28/75

*1975*

**ZORBA'S SUICIDE**

Zorba tried to commit suicide by hanging, himself from the towel rack in the bathroom, but the dog intervened by licking the tiles, and smiling with content animosity, His curious look elapsed into the time belt, and the clock talked back. Zorba dealt with his death like soggy toilet paper. Nothing could be grasped but the look behind the eyes. Nothing could be handled except the flowing juices in his brain. Zorba had cut off his toes three years ago in an attempt to murder his wife. Zorba yelled across the yard, "Leave me, and leave me alone to sweat in the cabbage field."

7/28/75

**A...**

A simple Siamese seagull,
playing games beneath the sand.
A robot sailing with inside-out teeth,
talks of running to Tucson,
or taking a laxative
to produce an altered state of mind.
A broken futsy doll,
licks the soft braids
of sweet doubt,
and swallows the seasons
of glass-blown tongues.
& silver button,
has a face that squeegees
the television into a bowling ball.
a bowling ball exists
in the invisible cloud,
of tomorrow's wash.
A time that is
thrown against the clock,
dissects itself,
like all the walnut butter
that sticks to the wall.

7/31/75

## BIRDS WEARING SHARKSKIN SUITS

If a bird wore a sharkskin suit,
he'd pee across the wind into a box,
that is labeled cornflakes, and beer.
Wax ears speak to rosebuds, that only envelope
themselves, like grape vine,
        like plastic baggies,
        like torn dolls,
who are not alone,
but lay docile
beneath the bleachers,
where soft butts
stare at the dirt.

7/31/75

## GLASS

Tomorrow the rain slips through the sieve to fill the cup of white birds. A black star is the eye of the television madness. Grape sorrows stain purple the blood of hungry hounds that flee on the run from consolidated diplomats. Angry wasps drink tea out of wax bags, while angels kiss the daring night, while angels bleed the soft glass morning. Aghast in the wind, a break in the glass is all there is to tell, what was going on in the wall. Who spoke the words of limerick romance to beetles in the grass? Raindrop madness scolding the pencil air! Frolic no more, beneath the dust on the floor or eat no raisins, while riding in boxcars. Homer died in a fit, eating his thumbs, eyeing all the angel junkies, with spears hurling their hearts and swallowing a glass of water to reach into itself for some relief, but found that all that has been tested, has been forgotten.

7/31/75

*1975*

**A DREAM**

A dream in the blackened night
of nine swords piercing your laughter.
Enter your soft frail buttocks of dreams.
A scream of nightmarish rose is eating your feet.
Awaken and hold on to the bloody bird corpse,
who stabbed himself when the depot closed?
Who slew the face of the clouds
and who took his head leaving the bloody stump
to sing to the black birds?

8/1/75

## SWORDS

Blindness unfolds in the hand of justice
and bleeds the soft air of her spirit,
that is glass that is frozen
in the electric exactness of bleeding iron.
The moon is made of wax.

Pierce the bleeding heart beneath the rain.
Pierce all the sundry dreams
and fill the empty spaces
with salt and wind.
Pierce the soul with a triple bladed sword
and blacken out the sun with clouds.

Cast yourself in a grave.
Look at death with mirror eyes,
with glass flesh and a fish shall be pierced
with a golden needle.

There is a tiger on the mount
licking his paws.
The water of the bay.
There are backs turned.
The people are faceless
and wear no grins
as does the tiger.

Dawn on the tears does not look back
but furrows on in a boat of jade,
with its listing passengers of sad sorrow
that carries with them as baggage
six swords
One for blood,
one for flesh,
one for' bona,
one for sight,
one for breath,
one for a calling tongue.

Dance with the silver swords,
dance with your boats of lace,
dance into the glass eye beating.
Feel the feet move

*1975*

and smile at all the laughing tents.

Dance, dance, dance.
Eight swords cage a lady in bondage.
If she bleeds, she wants.
If she lowers her tongue, she flees on broken toes.

8/1/75

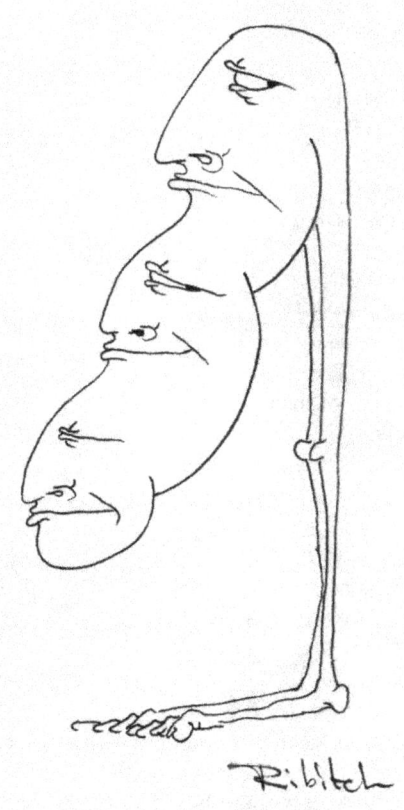

**TAROT
(INCOMPLETE)**

KING OF PINNACLES
The goat has become your left shoulder,,
Batting away at your heart.
Your robe of grapes has soured
and the wine in your flask
has turned to blood.
It is the blood of your hungry visitors,
each of whom is your brother.

ACE OF PINNACLES
I have stood in a garden of roses
and let my smile taste the sky.
From a cloud came a hand
that held the heart of the sun.
The breathing moment of life,
Leaves grew from my hand.
A flock of eagles
proceed from my mouth,
leaving my tongue
as a fertile branch in the wind.

PAGE OF PINNACLES
Who seconds their voice,
a giant holds his pinnacles erect,
gazing past future distances
into the jaded ring of the planed hand.
Oh, bleed yourself.
Oh, look beyond your fertile glance
and chip the glass wings of stone birds.

KNIGHT OF PINNACLES
A warrior in glass armor,,
A death mask of frozen daylight.

QUEEN OF PINNACLES
Your throne has a goat's head
with its tongue blazing in your lap.
The queen's eye is made of black marble
and reflects all the serpentine blue flash
of what sits before here
She has eaten all that she possesses

*1975*

and vomited all
that she desires.

KNIGHT OF SWORDS
Oh you bloody warrior wielding death.
On your horse of satin dream,
lick your swords after beheading the ghost of your sex.

QUEEN OF SWORDS
Is there mercy in your hand,
when your sword bleeds like a butchered cow.
Grant me to pass without exacting my toes
and don't set your dogs loose,
for they taste my flesh and drink my wine.

KING OF SWORDS
Sit by your queen,
she haunts you like a stallion
who is bleeding.
Sit by your queen,
for she beheaded your son
with the full of the moon.

ACE OF SWORDS
From the swift clouds came the hand
of leveling justice and took the heart
with the wreath
and bled the soft morning where crickets sing.


8/1/75

## PINNACLES

Infinity rages sport on the axis of the world.
Lick all the glances of Yin and Yang,
like all the bird wings that unfold on the continuous horizon.
A bleeding moment heads on forever in the juggler's hand.

The bishop tires of a moment of the herald
into the spastic cosmos of three-lettered pinnacles
of fifteen points, of mutable romance of the spirit touching itself.

The page who sits his assumed holiness above his head.
His holiness is placed next to his heart.
His holiness is under his feet, staring intently into the crossed eyes
of fathomless readers, like a gaze of triptych puzzlement.

Let the lessons be learned.
Five in the window where beggars torment the snow.
This is where swollen feet linger
and speak of forever journeys into the soul,
into the blazing torment of lead rain,
Five pinnacles bleeding under the soft light of their harmony.

Give a beggar a coin in measured condolences,
then weep at your own feet that are wrapped in cloth, and have birds sit on them.
Bleed them, and only then see past your blindness and into the beggar's palms.
What grows on my vine?
Black birds! Black birds who fly away after being watered, funneled, and cut from the vine.

What sees past the lust of wine and into its meager hand?
The tiller with his speck of gold, his eye of rabbit's fur and his neck of marble.
What bleeds from the sky?
A tender grape that is eaten by the boots of toil, that enraptures a foot made of lace.
Ah, craftsman of an ancient and lost art, feel your fingers grasp your tool,
to face the mirror on your soul, then piece together the remnants
of false products and nail them to their assess.

## 1975

A woman stands with her breast full.
The bird she holds is made of ivory.
I speak to her of faint roses, of strong smells that linger in the air
of frozen glance.
The woman turns into a river that runs away.
There is an old wizard
that is surrounded by dogs.
The dogs have eaten his hand.
Now handless he peers weakly in his age
at the phosphorescent memory of his fingers.

8/2/75

## VIEW FROM THE STAR SHIP

A wax parakeet holds no particular smile,
while riding atop a flag ship; a star ship,
and the black and blue night sky swallows
all the differences between glass and steel.

Robots sing sweet melodies, passing through rainbows,
in platinum exteriors, extinguishing each star in its turn,
diminishing the sky, and blacking out the universe.

100 Zumba drums penetrate the cosmos
bleeding their aching feet, and calling out the tongues
in the chill black night.

Phosphorescence in the lips of the moon,
sighing the calamities of blissful moments,
while riding on the back of a tongue, while riding on
the time tick of a moment.

Seeing glass eggs reflect the eternal cosmic creation,
the yellow heart sphere, the sun, set in hollowed hands,
the beat heart, rhythm dance, and bust of the flame,
baking the crust, floating amber ale.

Reflection of a mirror, in tight filled water bottle,
bleeding all the stones, where rivers touch the bear legs
of treacherous monkeys, who have the light in their head,
and mouthfuls, of raisin honey.

Casting long shadows, that disappear
off into the gravel night, where bears choke the wind,
releasing all the termites that eat the hooves of Pegasus,
who without a lamp stumbles blindly in the torn eaves,
who bleeds in darkness, and has no name.

The pure ink of midnight over the shallow beds of roses,
resurrecting the swan crosses that grow out of hands,
reaching for the tide flow of mangling touch.

Flags and drapes adorn the silk bodies of angels with no ears,
and melodious tunes speak from tubeless radios,
eating the transistor heart, flapping wings to desert air,
and breathing flame on phosphorous night.

*1975*

The tongue stretched horizon, builds monument tombs
of soft willow, and ash.
The gray whale eats at dinners reserved for pelicans,
and all their lust embedded into the fiery night.

8/3/75

**DREAMING AT NIGHT**

Resting on a bed of tallow
where dreams flicker
in the blue flame of night,
sucking all the windows
and the faces that
see through them.

Night's sweet pillow
of ostrich dreams,
of blanketed powerful wetness,
of flying without wings
in the astral body
of time stripped clean.

Who are the hunters?
who scream out in the night?
Their prayers for a successful killing
and the bird they hunt
are all within the sky,
where hands unfold
from the clouds, dreaming pipes,
and thistles are puncturing
the eyes of deadened dogs'
hungry wail.

8/13/75

## QUESTIONS

"Who has one they cried.
No answer was given.
The soft moon bled on their feet,

"Who needs one?" they asked.
and only the bleeding moon reached
to cup them in its hands.

There was no answer to any needing question.
Only the moon's soft grayness
to touch the earth
and steal the words from their mouths.


8/13/75




## WHERE POETS LINGER

Where poets linger in the flame.
Where flame eats the fingers of pen-wielding monsters,
that resembles language-built verse.
Screaming laughter where clouds linger as fingers protrude.
As a mouth's hungry warning lights up the sky
to feel itself dipped in mercury like so many dimes lost in the pocket.


8/13/75

*1975*

**WINDOWS**

There are windows in your forehead,
where birds peek out, where their beaks
speak the words of clocks, and cry out names
of dead poets, who dream themselves
out into blank darkness of hollowed caress.

Tongues stand erect, fondling
the wet wind and wings, they have none,
only sweet whispers of the indigo moon
having breakfast with the swift moving eggs of delight,
where owls parade their claws resembling fingers
and maids of yearning possess the warm touch
of quickened night and black asphalt.

Bears' teeth try to bite at wandering feet, and passing lullabies.
No senile flesh embarks to where rivers stem,
to where the sky runs on hurried wings,
and blankets all of dawn's lasting rays of light.
Speaking to angels that have been lost on the ground,
lost without their halos, and beaming light.
Castles stand with no one attending the grand gala balls,
with its rich laughter, lingering in the haze of pillowed morning.
Cities made of crystal and factories made of memory,
speak loudly where all the vines are overgrown,
and seeking out their destinies, in a single flaming match.

8/13/75

*Ribitch: The Last Word, Volume 1*

**L'AMOUR FOU, THE MAD LOVE**

L'Amour Fou,
the mad love,
desires, desire,
to touch all heavenly bliss
above silken clouds.
The stream of madness delight,
the cosmic revelation,
of L'Amour Fou,
the mad love,
the touch of desire
beneath the clouds,
the touch of desire
above the clouds,
voices singing,
singing to all the lovers,
who feel themselves
as the blue light,
the exciting blue flash.

L'Amour Fou,
L'Amour Fou,
the mad love,
the dreams of delight,
the dreams of desire,
desire beyond,
beneath the well,
sipping water,
sipping wine,
to the lips
of all the lovers
who are singing
melodies to the sky,
to the birds,
to the sparkling spring,
in all harmonious voices.

L'Amour Fou,
L'Amour Fou,
the mad love,
the flash of sparkle fresh,
the sweet smell
of jasmine's breath,

*1975*

with wings of ebony,
with eyes of ivory love.

L'Amour Fou,
the mad love,
the pure breakfast
at dawn,
the holy eyes
of desire's touch.
Today is singing,
the soft freshness
of newborn egg shells,
lifting the sun
with its eyes,
with its tongue,
above the stars.

L'Amour Fou,
L'Amour Fou,
the space in the
eye of lovers,
the lips of madness sublime.
L'Amour Fou,
the mad love,
the blue sparkle
that sets in the eye,
that speaks for itself,
in blindness,
to all hypocrisy's tongues.

L'Amour Fou,
the blue flame
that burns eternally
in sacred bliss,
that flies,
with birds of jade,
and ebony stars,
blood of the moon
bleeds soft memories
of delight,
of desires, desire,
of moments crying
in the hand of the sun.

L'Amour Fou,
delightful love,
love, love,
spontaneity of freshness,
space becomes the stars,
the stars their sister,
spring forth in fragrant
seas of timeless suns.

L'Amour Fou,
the mad love,
the springboard
on eternity,
love sings madness,
on desires, sublime.
O' let letters sing
alphabetical melodies,
open to the wind,
open to the spittle voice
of holy breath.

L'Amour Fou,
the mad love,
blue sparkle flash,
blue light of heavenly splendor,
excite the wind
with wings of armadillos,
sing freshness,
sing melodies,
of forgotten radios,
time is a spineless clock,
a timeless time,
built in love,
above all rich laughter,
polling with the thunder,
baying at the moon,
as the moon bays
at the lovers,
entwined on the sand.

L'Amour Fou,
the mad love,
the singing rhinoceros
wears a bow tie

*1975*

for the wedding
of the sun and the moon.
Glass eagles' flight
carry them over
many threaded needles,
talk of silence
in a dark room,
where the smells
of desire flower,
into desire's desire.
O' love,
mad love,
blue flash,
light of love.

L'Amour Fou,
L'Amour Fou,


8/16/75



**SITTING WITH FRIENDS**

A moment sitting with friends,
the crocodile,
the armadillo,
the wart hog,
all the space that is between them,
is no more than the air
that floats in the sky,
Like all the eyes
that wink,
and like all the lovers
that embrace
in the soft moon,
oh love,
oh love between them all.


8/16/75

## THE MADONNA OF FROZEN DREAMS

The Madonna of frozen dreams, speaks turtle tongues
to all the spacious multitudes.
Breaking all the winds that are in the salamander's eye,
sparkles like the frost dew of gracious wedding feast.
The glass hogs, wail in the wallow of muddy dreams.
Water sits, waist deep, where my neck grows, like weeds in the frost.
A wax dummy melts itself into the floor,
resembles a dog biting its tongue in the morning.
A mask of plaster, cracks in the dust of filtered romance.
Looking into the mirror, I see my face,
it feels like a rose, lifting above the frozen ground.

8/27/75


## THE SPACE INSIDE

The space inside,
the electric egg
is the cosmic eye,
that revolves inside
the doll,
that eats at the sky.
The glass rose
is a space pilot,
in the conquering haze,
of leaves following the rainbow's
flash of light,
enveloping the lost horizon.
Spin the sun
on your fingers,
spin your eyes,
in the faucet wind
of melodious smile.

8/27/75

*1975*

## THERE ARE MOMENTS

There are moments, in the weather vane
where a spontaneous interlude of gracious light,
breaks the silence with an ivory fist.
Jaded crows, who in their wanderlust
evoke the tempers of needless angels.
Boneless skeletons, who in their presence
speak of dead wood, on stone houses.

Timeless, as a cloudless sky, the end all is at their feet,
in the dry dust of a sorrowful morning.
A bleak cinder is inside the eye, a cold reminder
of souls lost and wrapped in doilies of blood.
Warped, and bleeding, the wings of frail birds,
fly into the horizon's mechanical dreams.

No forward in time.
No sweet breeze to wipe the wind.
Oh, response of the dawn under the wing of flies,
wrapped in cellophane, like crisp dollars of false screams.
Oh, a moment in latitude's romance,
silken in its harmony, silken in the wave of gray ash,
of the sea, at the moment, of the spontaneous dawn.

Silver sea fish parade
with the willow freshness of spring's dance.
A toad turns into a far sighted man, eating all the flesh
from the apples of weary suns.
Cross yourself in the holy bathroom of your years.
The blessed the toilet has eyes of multiple romance,
Tied off into the waiting mouths of forever elating a scream.

Oh, web of spider's sorrows entangling the breath
of giants bleeding, of giants looking out of eyes,
that see the hidden horizons on the radio flesh.
Oh, break the toast over the head of the ostrich's praying,
of feet buried deep into the hands of naked beaches.
Rabbits run, into the sea of tears, crossing themselves
with swollen glances, and no perfect slivers of robot shivers.

8/28/75

## FIGURE CUT FROM PAPER

Who cut the figure of
a desiccated moose in half?
To take out its belly
and turn it into gold.

Fry its face in fish oil.
Place an alphabet on its teeth.
Oh, castle
of castration
and blind Buddhist pudding.

Rest the fall, of Rome.
On a dime.
On a quarter of meat,
of uneducated violence,
of overeducated violence,
of dolls quivering
in stale bathrooms.

Tomorrows of times lost
in the hollow dream
of spastic romance.


9/11/75

*1975*

## THE GLASS MEMORY

The memories can't
be denied
in the glass
that returns
a look into the eyes.
Spanking the wind
with a copper belt
and trailing the poor
soft drunks
who press themselves
to the bar stools
with whores' lips
and the glass
stands empty,
empty as the fool's
tears that gaze
into the glass
to see hazy memories.


9/12/75

## A BLACK SPARROW YEARNING

The soft mood night, strips its blouse to reveal its crow's breast, and its black blood, doted on the tongue of screaming sight. A woman stands on a small mound, under the cleft of the moon, her eyes have been plucked by the wind, and she wears a blindfold over her sightlessness. She weeps through the cloth. She holds in her hands, a few straws of wheat, and a burnt tree.

Off in the distance, a dinner is being served, and the raucous laughter splinters the air, and bakes the sky's blood. The woman on the mound has been crucified for overabundant thought, and for her sightless rage. Her thighs are stapled with roses, the thorns pled with her wedding to the frost. Her hair matted with burrs, her sex sewn shut. Her lips hold a regaled tongue. Her folding romance lies at her feet.

Eagles that are wingless have no beaks of gold, no breathe nor wires connecting the eyes to radios. The laughter becomes stone, a lead weight hung about the neck of the next severing sword. The bleeding heart, where the tongue lies on the floor, speaks jealousies to the floor boards.

9/13/75


## I SAT ALONE

I sat alone
in the corner of the waste basket
itching the frozen shadows of dream
where once I bled,
where once I tumbled,
where twice I heard laughter.
The monocle hovers in space
with one eye fixed on lead feet.
No afterthought entwined,
no barracuda lost in
fever touch of
Arabian gold.

1/9/75

*1975*

## DETESTED FLAGRANCE OF SHALLOWNESS

Adorn the walking jackal,
with mired jewels
of beaded sweat,
let the tongue
of angry swallows
flay with bloody whips,
the backs of saddened clowns.
Those who sit backward
in their carriages,
with aprons on,
with teeth of gold,
with all the green scales.
The mountain has
taken all of its dust,
labored its face
into sweetened
sun-scorched eyes.
The heat of baked days
is angry at
the bleached faces
of walking women,
who wear evening gowns,
and plastic jewelry.


9/27/75

## I MIGHT HAVE COME FROM SPAIN

The precious cargo teeth, assailed the mired wind in alligator suit, tuxedo breath, and jumbled tiger's harmony. Who cut off their fingers for the tortoise, stripped in the morning frost? Bite the tail of running madly. Eat the flesh of undressed clowns. Fire upon the naked beach, where gulls lay, stripped of their heads, and soaked in oil. Offering to the sand, the bleeding grain of ambiguous nosebleed, soft chains, glass hearts and melodies play on a tuneless harpsichord. The tunnel is blocked with fecal membranes of stuffed freight trains. Ok, leopard spots on the back of silver fingers eat the burnt toast of yesterday's yearning, and sneaks past the covered booths, where jackals beat off to the rock rhythms of no music bands. An eggshell holds all the tomorrows in hands of white ivory. A ship of eyes sails for Spain, where I used to live where I used to take a pen in swollen hands, to speak to all the covered corpora.

9/27/75


## "OF"

A rocket jet of spurting jizum,
that covers the whole
wheat bird of life,
of silver taste,
of angel breath,
that confirms the
senile romance
of fingers and feet,
of time and no time,,
of blasting powder
and naked dawn,
the silent Moses
who wears a gown
of black gold
and bleeding hearts.

9/28/75

*1975*

**ROBOT**

A robot made out of tin, made out of jelly,
with no wires for a tongue,
and coins bleed from the electric eyes.
My planet, of foam touches the moving vehicles,
of automatic wipers and suppressed eyelids.
Planet foam is asking no questions
of lead dummies, who melt down their brains for silver.

9/28/75

**APPLE OF YOUR THROAT**

The evening table stands beside a pool of water, and the telephone rings the stagnant blue bird whistle. A load of cherries speaks of their trees at a public address meeting. There are old bubbles in the sink. A fish watches the late show. An open wound, looks like the Holland tunnel at dusk. A rich woman pirates a bus to downtown in a hurry, wearing platform shoes and eating water lilies. Open a flask at dawn... Who is your spiral staircase in tow with a nosebleed and with a wormhole in the apple of your throat.

10/1/75

## OPEN THE SALAD OF YOUR MIND

The evening table stands beside a pool of water, and the telephone rings the stagnant blue bird whistle. A load of cherries spoken of their tree, at a public address meeting. There are old bubbles in the sink. A fish watches the late show. An open wound looks like the Holland Tunnel at dusk. A rich woman pirates a bug to downtown in a hurry, wearing platform shoes. Eat water lilies. Open a flask at dawn. Who is spiral staircase now with a nosebleed with a worm hole in the apple of your throat.

10/1/75

## SPLIT OPEN A HOUSE

There was a dawn of red film, that is collected in the air, like a magnet of malignant roses. The dust hovered on the landscape, explaining itself in the swallowed spring. A woman appeared holding a chestnut mare. She had at last severed her belly, and stepped slowly out of her maze. She spoke softly? "Let me introduce you to....," She cut off her words with silver scissors, and stuffed them inside a bag that sat beside the chestnut mare. "My chestnut mare," she continued, muffling from out of the bag. She stood on a tea bag that was bloody with worth. She spawned herself in a leper's tongue of relief. A bird came out of crystal sky, and alit on the horse's back. It was a hummingbird. The bird flew off with the horse. She watched, as three men came out of a hole in the sand. They each had on suits. They each had a bleeding wound on their hand. "My horse just flew away with a hummingbird," she said.

"That happens," they replied.

10/1/75

*1975*

## I THREW IT INTO THE SEA

I threw it into the sea
and it turned into a pelican
and flew away.
It became empty.
The loss of it confused me.
The sea raged at my feet.
I felt a quick swallow in my throat,
I could not get it down.
I bled in the sand
and became a quick grain.
Look at me now,
am I alright?

10/2/75

## NOBODY HEARS

You feel empty
when nobody
sees your voice,
when you become invisible,
when your nakedness
is not of any importance.
If your mirror breaks
and nobody picks
up the pieces
and you look at yourself
and see only dying pelicans
and rusty locks.

10/4/75

## THE BLACK EYED FISH OF SILENCE

The black eyed fish of silence
mellows the breath
of fish-like continuities.

The swallow sings of spring,
        the fresh daisy
                sips wine with Frenchmen.
        Is that ok?
        Is that the stone trick?
To find space in the wind,
        to fly the robust smile,
oh' fragrant
mist that swallows
        itself at dawn.
oh' break open
        the leaves of fresh loaves,
                fresh loaves, stale moons.

10/5/75

## TIME CLOCK

I have no watchfulness in my time clock.
I am the wizard of eternity, over and over again
Severed in the brainless clock on my death,
that resembles even my dust.
My whole empty body that squeezes
out of a lemon peel, like blood from my wrist,
My eyes are looking inside the backwardness
of my head that you won't ever forget.
Do you think I am a crotch of anger?
Fingering all those times that I am in doubt.

10/5/75

*1975*

**A SONG FOR THE SLEEPER**

Who committed an audacious act,
beneath a balloon,
filled with the hot breath
of a dying sun,
a sun of a thousand names?
who sips wine
in the parlors of gilded romance
with the panicle of thieves,
who in their own open
belief, sang to the tortoise
of soft believing,
and wept with the sun?
who was alone
on the panicle of dreams?
who sat with all
the fresh fishers,
of dreams,
and ate with all
the bleeding dreams,
for the dreams themselves,
sing for the sleeper?


10/24/75

## NIGHT

The night soaked
the sky with a sponge,
ate the lettuce face
of monkeys running,
on the hollow,
on the fire built
breath of day,
that roasts the blue wind,
O' sky,
bleed again,
in the dust,
in the blackest night.

10/24/75

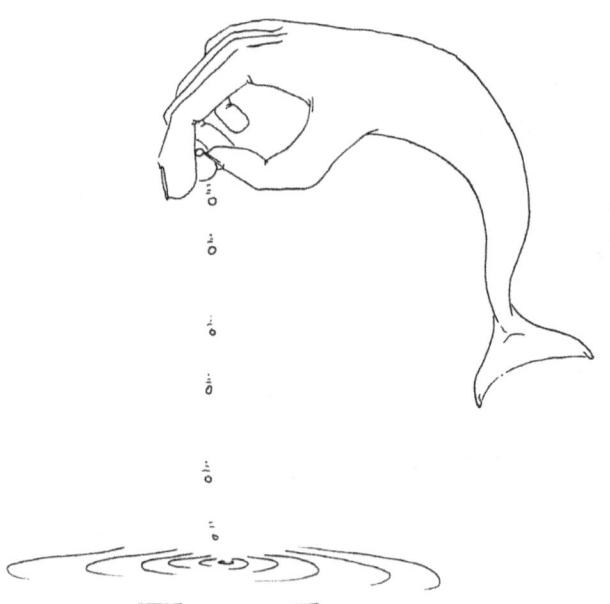

*1975*

**SPANISH DUST**

The hermetic wind,
romances, the soft sand pillows
on your dream,
like a knife in flesh that bleeds,
like the wind-forming tallow.
There is a beast, who claims his name,
who bleeds all his moments,
like a sweet deer
slain with a dagger of ivory.
A hopeless runner
has severed his legs,
and thrown apart the jealous wind.
Split an apple with teeth of blood,
and oil the only fragrant blast,
that sees itself feeding
in the moldy horizon,
with translucent bears,
and bloody wings
of your hands.
Your eyes stare into
the candle-scent dream
of morbid pallor,
and only the tongues
of flying madly,
open to the fresh eye of the wind,
stays aloft for a while,
when the songs of Spanish
dust, sip the soft embers
of frail love.

10/24/75

## THE DAY THAT BIRDS BURNED

The day that birds burned
their flame-like legs spread open to the wind.
The day that birds burned,
they bled off in the open, split their bellies on the open tram,
and split upon the tracks their electricity.
The day that birds burned,
their faces' mirrored flame, and all the hope
that they mired set upon the dust ash of their soft brains.
The day that birds burned,
they called out to hope, and hope fled them.
They stood wasted, in their cloth dreams,
aflame in their tongues.
The day that birds burned,
they sang in chorus, the blood songs of their wedding,
and feasted in the fated remembrance of swollen
eyes that set upon the flame.
The day that birds burned,
there was a grace in the air, a blood on the foot,
and a fire that sat in the eyes of fine ash dust.
The day that birds burned,
they filled their wine glasses, with flame,
and drank a toast, to the center of the sun.


10/24/75

*1975*

## THE SCALDED FISH

There are leaflets of glass upon the eyes
of supposed mythology, where the lips of women
mingle on the corners of smiles and lament.
An ostrich screams in rage and swallows the booth
of split dreams.

Opalescent eggshells, run for taxis, on the avenues
of continuous sorrow, where the winds of disbelief
take despair by the wing, and wrestle
with the fires of silver blood.

Women smile at the cement roses, or a face of angelic dreamers.
They place themselves inside the lover's abdomen,
to sip the fiery semen of eyeless blood.
A blanket scorns the flannel pajamas, that scold the daylight,
of incandescent flight.

The smile of rooted-in fragrant fly-pillows
told the wretchedness of the swallow's dawn or in the suckling moon,
that hovers where only the rose bleeds itself,
past the black eyed draper, that hangs onto the pointed penis,
that pierces the hungry arm.

There is a smile on the back of the hand,
And a broken radio speaks to all
the frozen walls.


10/24/75

## WAITING

The walker into the pudding,
waits,
waits,
sitting alone on a wooden bench,
smoking a cigarette,
and counting all the swollen cracks
in the walls,
or in the face of madmen.
The freedom that they lost,
they left behind
in an empty can.
The bleeding soft night,
lingers in the light,
waiting for forever,
to come in on a bus,
to come in on a flight from Spain,
or to die in the tile
designs of a hungry mood.
The seer of beauty,
wakens to the song
of the dawn,
and flees on blistered feet,
to the rear of the compartment,
where blind energy
burns the hand
of waiting beggars.

10/24/75

*1975*

## A BLACKENED SPEAR
## OF ANGEL TONGUES

Soft epileptic angels
knead the plastic dough
of senseless breaded
caressing all fragrant roses,
and mingling all
the faces of lead pudding,
of glass revolvers.

Blatant dream,
of egg-faced lopsidedness,
an inside-out face
of dream,
of apple reluctance,
of unseen invisibilities,
that eats away
at the moon of gypsies.

Ah, scent of frozen wolves,
that eats the sun,
with bowls of cherries,
and ionize dust
mingles with the general's face,
his gun,
his blackened tongue,
of lead,
of luckless ice.


10/25/75

## PRESIDENTIAL PROFANITIES

The axe came down on the nation that fed fools.
Their glass military gem indeed died.
They ate their money with a host of eagles
Then planted the seed of their blood
Into the polluted beaches of their sorrow
They knew nothing of the braced lamp
That burst in their hand
That screams for no light and no dream
The sanity fled with broken legs
They all believed it was
They all saw their diarrhea leader
Split open at the seams like a rag doll
Entering into his mansion of madness
To contemplate the war
To shoot his brains out.

10/25/75

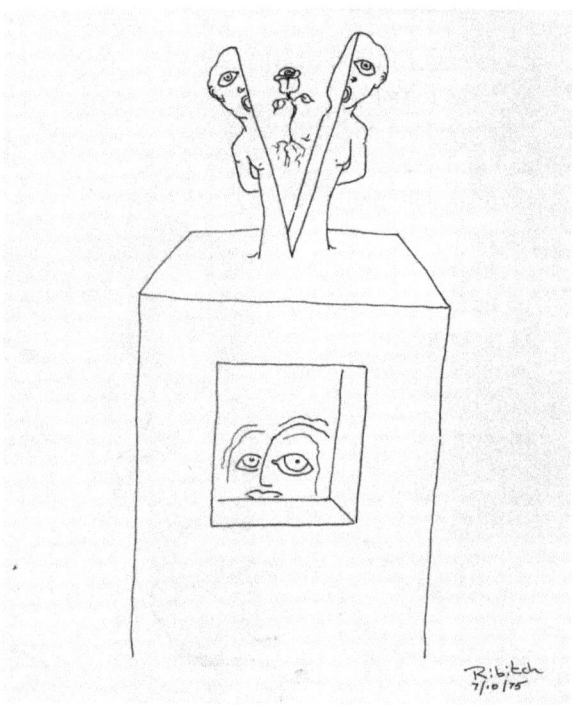

*1975*

**PRISON DUST**

The precious moment
inside the clock,
where all the gray monkeys
see they are lost.

They fill all the spaces
inside the cell of locked corridors.
This place is bleeding,
for all the prisoners,
who wait inside their napkins,
and feel the felt faces,
that press inside the stomach fate.

False bars,
and cement floors,
where ancient maggots play,
a rosebud romance takes place
with all the tools of the heart,
and with feelers of the
frozen throat.

A black eyed priest
stabs the padded moon,
inside of a boat,
that is aflame.
The pregnant moment
sets to sea
on an open hand,
with a pistol of rage.


10/25/75

**I HOLD THE SUN**

I hold the sun
that I present to you
in my cupped hands.
The warmth of days
on the mellow grass,
where my lips touch
your forehead
to kiss the spot
of the moon.
To sing soft
lullabies in your ear.
Listen to the hand
of my heart
as it caresses
the softness of your cheek
and play with
the soft moods
of our love.


11/13/75

*1975*

**SWEET LIPS**

Let sweet lips
touch the fondled
buds of our eyes.
Ah, again to be
the sun that I
always was.
Fleeting on the sand
like licking
all the fragrant
mist of day.
That is
in the soft
fingers
of the sun's
reaching arm.

11/18/75

**I STEP INTO THE LEAVES OF MY LIFE**

   I step into leaves of my life, touching all the spaces, with my eyes, that are made of wood, that are made of black jade. There are moments that are spent kissing the clouds, touching all the spaces that are in colors of the rainbows, and looking out for golden strands to a harp that sits in the palm of my hand.
   The wind that is the deep feeling in chest, is flying like great birds, singing, songs to the sable sun, and leaping like a frog's eye, out beyond the smile of the sky. I in a hundred different parts, each going here, and there, each love, a moment, a year, each walking with soft feathers and talking the round and flat places in my feet. So with great pleasure I sing like all corners of my mind, and laugh with all the lightness that is within me.

12/3/75

## PIECING TOGETHER THE STARS

To piece together the stars, where I love you,
to see into the spaces of the labyrinth of stolen eyes.
The birds have voices made of ivory, made of silver love.
The sky touches the lips that part in eternal kiss,
separating the moon from all the stars that play beyond the eye.
Felt skin on felt skin, playfully singing wordless romance to the sea.

A cloud of dust that is your eye that is your tender touch of silk.
A milkiness that takes over, the spread seed of our delight.
A spoken word that lays silent in our touch.
The rays of the moon bleed themselves together in a continuous bliss,
together we play soft tunes for our ears that run together
in the fragrant grass of our smiles.

you are the feet that walk, your face meets mine in the window beyond the mirror.
We each know the other's face, by all the light of a single candle.
Soft wind upon our lips, cools the spaces of love in the starry night.
Let us speak when our mouths join, let the stars bless our heads
and let the moon kiss the black night, and the pearled eagle of splendid moments.

You are the word love, and the moment of dream.
You are cascading moments of touch and speak with a fine jeweled voice.
And I,
       and I,
              fly at the tip of your wings, tasting your fire.


12/6/75

*1975*

## AFRICAN NIGHTS

Sweet honey of the moon,
tastes the African night's
sweet taste,
and magnificent dance
of jeweled gazelles.
The harbor of sweet memory,
the flavorful tongue,
the eye jade of the sea.
Sweet African nights,
wail in the breeze,
the songs of love.
The black star
wraps its arms
around the swirling
cavity of the shiftless mood.
Black African nights,
sweet basil of dreams.
Dust of gold honey.
Flight of starry air,
filled into the sleep
of elephant herds.
The soft spoken tongue
of the waves,
touches long African nights,
with its angled hair trees,
and black African nights,
of sweet Congo moon.
Blast hot furnace on skin
tanned velvet touch on skin,
the bleeding lion,
the soft moon,
skin on skin,
sweet hot on hot,
melted butter,
the sun sinks into the sea,
where African nights
eat the pillows of dreams.
The long yellow corn
neck of singing giraffes,
meets the sky with tongue,
and magnificent slow grace.
African nights,

full of diamonds,
full of the screaming
birds of love.
African nights,
hollow in the breeze,
soft in the romantic mood
of fingers touching lips.
Hat skies weep,
to flavor the ground
of Swazi kiss.
Fire of Bantu gods,
raise their curved fingers
to the sky,
touching black African nights,
leaving their fingerprints
in the black African heavens.
Africa, black, black Africa,
the midnight moon of jade.
Ah, black kiss of the sky,
touching the earth,
the rich African soil,
carved in it blackness and beauty,
where the night dances
with the hands of the moon,
touching all the velvet skin,
sweating in the heat,
dancing with midnight lagoons,
where fire fish sip their wine,
and talk of their beauty,
of their sweet basil African nights,
that swells in the hot summer heat,
waiting for the refreshing
dampness of a summer rain.
The night sticks out it claws,
like a panther, hungry upon the air,
to cut into the bleeding soil
that reaches to the river angry tongue.
Ah, African night,
not like any other night,
 not like any other,
for sweet black African night,
night of the Congo, night of the Swazi,
night of the Nqutu,
night of the Rwanda,

*1975*

night of the Zulu,
night of the Masai,
night of the blessed
naked darkness,
night the myth,
hot night of Africa,
night of the river's tongue,
where hippos play,
where the roar of its voice
speaks to the African air.
Night like no other, that breathe,
that lives with the stars.
The hand strokes
the present moon of desire,
Ah, the sweet present moon,
a diamond in the African night,
a rich glow upon the earth,
speaking songs of laughter.
The night speaks,
the night weeps and moans,
the night has silver fingers
to touch the grass of lion's hair.
That night,
longest of longest nights,
the soft tune of its pleasure,
the want of its desire,
where love is the warmth fire
of rivers meeting the sea,
in intertwining intercourse,
licking the flesh of the earth.
Ah, like no other night, like no other,
The blackness of dark honey,
the sweet basil of African nights.

12/17/75

**FOUNTAINS**

Fountains of gold and silver,
hair of cascading water,
love of pools,
and jade droplets.
Let me touch you
beneath the spray,
beneath the roaring lions.
In fountains of dream,
we fondle touch
of love's caress,
and run with the water
of moments of our dreams.
Fountains that speak
with rippling tongues
with the cool breeze
of our love,
with the fountain's splendor.
Fountains of love,
sprinkling our foreheads
with kisses of water,
and there we'll wade
out deep into the fountain's
crystal depth.


12/21/75

*1975*

## THAT EVENING SMELLS LIKE WINE

That evening smells like wine,
that touches my heart
with soul caress of the setting sun.
Ah, to touch you in that evening,
to find you beneath my pillow of dream,
Then out there beyond the horizon
with a flaming torch of a heart,
and the drumbeat of my living,
yes, that moment under the stars,
with the tender glass of eyes.
Running with the wind,
my legs moving faster,
my heart pumping
with each lift of the foot,
I cross over the mist of dream
and into the spacious volume
of love's immense treasure.

12/21/75

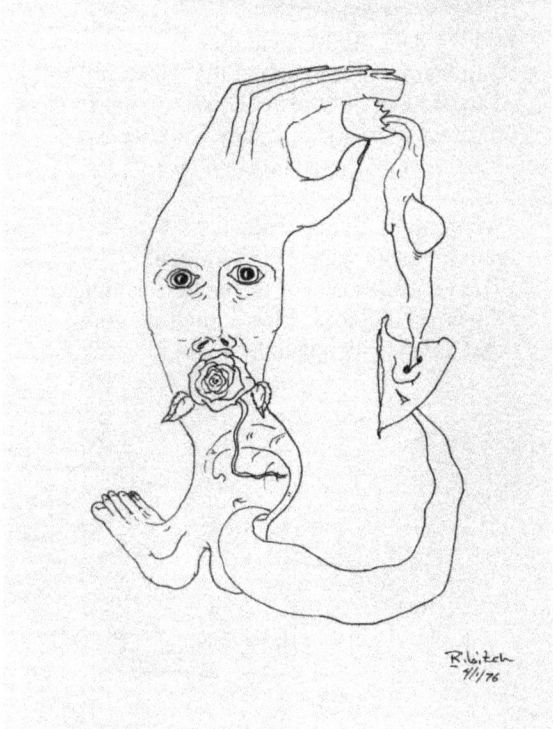

*Ribitch: The Last Word, Volume 1*

## WHERE DOES ALL THIS LEAD ME?

Where does all this lead me?
out beyond the dawn of a new day,
smelling like fresh orchids of elephants.
The sweet spray of a morning mist,
the sweet flight of wingless birds
going to roost in the palm of my hand,

Where does all this lead me?
into the darkness of untraveled caves.
The haunting smell of the night jasmine,
The high flying condor of lips,
that takes flight into my eye.

Where does all this lead me?
past the blue horizon of angel's fingers.
The harmonies of old radios in the night,
the cool blast of sweet air on the run,
that takes my nose by the feet.

Where does all this lead me?
into the palm of my hand that is flavored.
The deepness of the eye looking intent,
the soul of love that stands with the sun,
kissing at all the clouds that pass by.

Where does all this lead me?
into love, the wine of my tongue.
The velvet flowers of the hand touching,
the cream colored skies of melting glass,
that extends its lips to kiss you in the wind.

12/21/75

*1975*

**APPLE ON MY SKIN**

I open the apple on my skin,
to see the jade ostrich fade Into darkness,
fade into the bleeding prince of wanting.

There at the top of my face lingers
the swallowed droplets of water colored green.
I walked into, under, over, then into again,
      again...
      Ah, super, yes…
      Ah, super, yes…
Now speaking from a hole in the ground
that is filled in, that has a voice
speaking from out of it.
      Ah, super, yes...
      and no way to control it.

12/22/75


**CAGE OF ETERNITY**

The naked sun sees
eagles playfully
slitting the wrist
of tomorrow's sorrow
on a plate of silver eyes.
That time itself bleeds.
The moment is lasting,
as long as the sun
licks its death
from your brow.
Ah, gold lace,
lace of fevered blood.
That moment of fear
grips the hand,
as the thought,
to push the eager runner
to the cage of eternity.

12/22/75

## DANCE OF THE ROPE AND GALLOWS

There is blood on the wire, where the rope dances with the naked tear drop.
Eyes eat at the flesh of dangling feet, and mope in the shadows of frustrated sorrow.
The hangman tongue is split, and decorated with wreaths.
The rope dances on the eyes of hungry death.
The song licks their eyes, and picks out the dawn, for the trial's parade.
The stage is set, and the dance shall begin, with the rope's snap, and the neck's gentle gasp.
With feet touching the air and the rope is dancing to the richness of blood.
What hour of the execution wails on the soft night air, where the rope plays with sweet death on the neck? That hour has come, as has the dance of the rope.

12/22/75

## THE FACELESS NIGHT

The faceless night chases on scalded feet the moon who is Mood and the name of the cat. To freeze the hands at the palm, and the gray tip of the mouth, there in the midnight relief the tongue swallows the accent: of dimes, of flavored days, like the wind who is mad, like the scream from the throat of a gilded fish with a rhinestone stomach. All the places that are not on maps, but smell like geography, in there wailing mouths. There are birds that speak with black veiled condors that sit and wait for buses to take flight out beyond the moon.

12/22/75

*1975*

**SITTING IN A CAFE**

We sat in the cafe,
our fingers twitching
the rhythms of ancient drums.
We stared into the deep chasms
of our longing eyes,
our hair turned to fish,
and our faces in time
with the cook's ladle.
The table moved
with us still at our dinner,
we gave close pursuit
but lost sight of the vanishing
food in the vast horizon
of velvet wall hangings,
and plastic manikins.
We held our breath,
and each other's hand,
while the room shifted
in the darkness,
to become the robot
of the wind.
The waiter was lost
in his red pajama suit,
he was eyeing us,
thinking we would steal away,
without paying,
without leaving a tip.
The cafe reeked of madness,
the table walked
on our toes,
we talked lightly so as
not to upset our stomachs,
which had left the cafe
an hour ago.

12/22/75

## THERE ARE CASTLES BEYOND THE MOON

There are castles beyond the moon, with rose-colored windows,
and great herds of elephants painted on its towers.
There are stars that are eyes looking into the faint blue mist of morning.
The green flowers of faces, each owning a hand of love.
There are castles beyond the moon, beyond the tips of fingers,
out in the universe of flying whispers.
Mountains talk to rays in castles of jade crystal and of cinnamon honey.
There are castles beyond the moon, that has eyes of silver,
looking into the heart, where songs are sung, where invisible laces
are sewn in the darkness.

There are castles beyond the moon, and its shadows of eyeless faces,
that speak in the ear of delight.
There are moonbeams that make up the gowns of angels,
that make up beds of lovers.
There are castles beyond the moon, in its grace and wonder,
in its love and flicking tongue, that touches the sky,
that is felt, that is warmth that is graceful bowing, into my hungry heart.
You speak like sweet symphonies of green jade.
There is a soft pillow of your voice that lingers in the ray of sleep
in my thoughts.

There are soft pillows of my dream, that carries me to unseen depths,
where your love awaits, with fingers of calling birds.
l am a hunter, in the leaves of romance, and each way that I turn,
there is the soft music of your hair, and the sweet melodies of your eyes.
To embark on a journey of ivory, to see into the caverns
of the tender beast of love, where waits the waiting fingers of your
tongue.
You are the flying wings of circling birds, that collide with the sun,
and sip the juice of roses as the day melts into my hand.
My face meets yours where all the canaries free themselves from cages.
We are one in our hearts, and two in our souls, that fly free,
seeking the breezes of love's flight and being in love.

*1975*

There are castles beyond the moon, guarded by stars, and blue heavens.
There are moonbeams in your eyes, crystal clear and loving.
I smell the cool night, and rose fingers of light, the green faces of leaves,
the moments of dawn's love.

There are castles beyond the moon that lives in the stars
that lives in love that lives in my heart.
There are castles beyond the moon,
there are castles inside my love, inside your eyes.
There are castles beyond the moon, and in them lives romance,
live the soft colors of touch.
There are castles beyond the moon,
there are castles beyond the sun,
there are castles beyond the stars,
There are castles,
        and there are castles,
                and there are castles beyond the moon.

12/22/75

1976

## ANIMAL SUIT

I wear an animal suit
like the jumping eye
of my lute,
of rising crab claws
of daily delight.
Ah …a spiral glass of gin
to the top of the world,
of flying madly,
      madly,
              into the sky
of doubtful likeness
of the flying bird.


1/8/76


## I WALK THE PLATFORM

I walk the platform
on a gilded shoe,
we stare into
the black jade
of my finger
holding a pen
that bleeds
into the dirt
of my eye


1/8/76

*1976*

**THE SPACE BETWEEN THE EYES**

The space between the eyes
that haunts all
the fragments of days
zeroed in the
tropical
eye of the tongue.


1/8/76

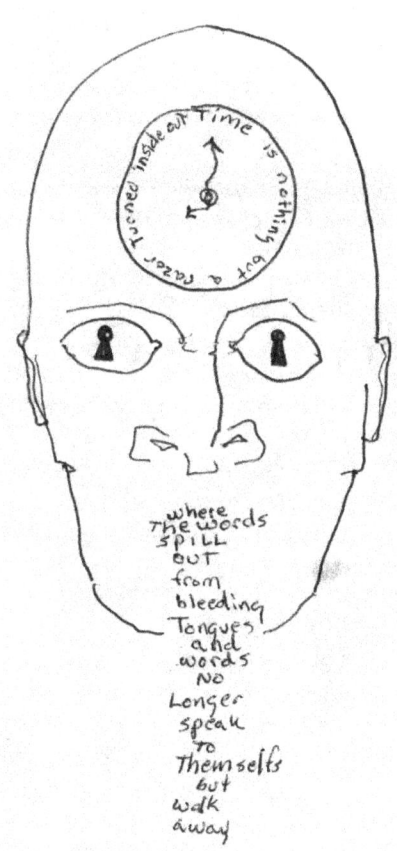

## A BLEEDING TEAR FOR A POET OF SPAIN
**(For Federico García Lorca)**

I have felt the gun against the wall,
the bullets that bleed and the soft morning that talks
to my sweet whispers in the Spanish night.
I spoke words into the air, into my people,
Into the muzzles of fire death.
The guard turned my face away, so as not to see
my death stare or hear the poetry that fell from my lips
like the wine that fell from theirs.
The palms of my hands bled the soft sorrows
of their bridges, and those bridges burn
the flame from my heart and they wish that only once,
that they could see fear tremble and my legs buckle.
They feared their own mirrors
and could not find enough tape to cover the cracks.
With guns at the ready, I felt my death was quite romantic.
When the rose wilts beneath their tears,
my lips move and my fingers play with the wind.
Like dust on the down of feathers,
I felt a multitude of words that caressed my tongue
and bled from my pin like the thin trail of blood down my chest.
I could hear the shot!
I could hear the swift death touch the rose of my life
And I tasted the soft dust on my blood-soaked tongue.
Now I have returned and my hot breath turns to fire.
My lips move and my tongue sizzles the taste of salt tears.
My mouth is never quiet and never shall it be.
Franco is dead and the People of Spain
do not weep and nor do they rejoice,
for the walls are bloody of their neighbors and sons
and their daughters still stand raped.
Franco is dead and I have returned.
The walls are red of death's blood
and the lines are getting longer, waiting for the muzzle.
If the line should contain me for death's second helping,
Then my lips shall move and the words on my tongue
shall be flame and they will BURN!

1/15/76

*1976*

## THE BASEMENT OF GLASS

Open the face of
the stagnant dungeons
where all the angels
have leprosy
and French kiss
the magnets of
their hands
and bleed
again in the
soft moon
of their delight
and their sorrow,
because the beak
of the bird
is silver
under the light.


1/15/76


## WHOLE LOT TO SEE

There is a whole
lot to see
fishing on the other side
of the face
with eyeglasses
and faint image
of the blue
transparent rose
that has a brain
of its own
to grab the wheel
on progress
and stretch it backward.


1/15/76

## OPEN TEARDROP

The open teardrop
into the resin sky,
with my lap
bleeding
in the soft mouth of tomorrow
bleeding also,
        oh yes also,
where the breakers beat on the open rushes of fiery timber line.

1/16/76

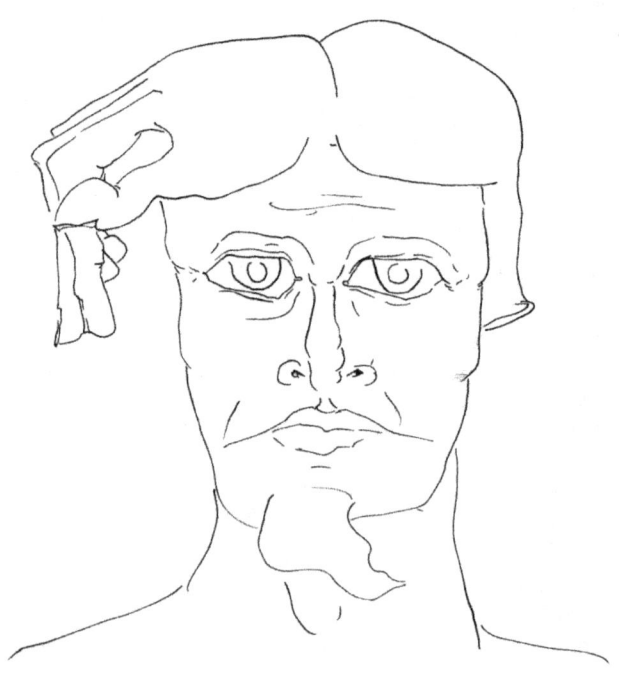

*1976*

**SECRET TUNNELS**

The secret tunnels burn the blue flame of their breath
on the wine glasses filled with remembered
faces and remembered guns.

The revolution's dying tears and the many faces
that wander the streets after darkness
counting the bricks that weep,
counting the walls that scream.

These are walls, bullet pock marked
and painted red from their dying grief.
The sad farewell, and the train is on fire,
its tongue flames and is set in swift water.

The anger cuts into the flesh like a swift knife
and its mouth like no fool, tears the bricks
of their bloody laughter and splinters the air
with its own malignant curses.

There in the pillowed dreams of awareness
in the spark of flame set from the guns of madness,
the fresh corpse of longing intently and the sweet tears
of disbelief entangle their fingers about the throat.

Stinging glances of ideas and the revolution bleeds
with all the stilled fingers, with all the quieted voices
that won't ever be quiet and the bodies of the executed
will never lay still as long as the blood
of their injustice bitters the mouths of those who remain
still imprisoned in the beast.

1/16/76

## CLOCK

The basket bleeds
the moment to seek
the apple moments
of the day.

       Is that right?

The moment is ok
a fine flame in the darkness
in the palm of my hand
like a razor blade sweeping
the sky with one bleeding
strike of the clock

1/17/76

## WHAT LAYS AT THE BOTTOM OF STREETS

   Into the wooden doors of Pegasus, an old face in the wind has cracked lips and smiles. Open the door in the mouth of my tongue where words execute the bleeding eyes of a nation's sorrow. The mast moans and cries the sirens that are the blood on their throat, where the cries of the city bleed in the soft morning. I moan the twilight of song, the ever reminiscent river of thunder. The backrooms of the years eat at the swallow tail of mannequin's yearning. The flesh of the wind stains the blood fear in the morning.
   Open the stretched palms to help slide into the eyes of fate and jack the pillows of the mind and melt the heated rays of the sun. Every person bleeds, either alone or in crowds. There are no more cotton swabs, only fresh pools.

1/17/76

*1976*

**MY PASSION EXTENDS**

My passion extends
a colored hand
into the heart
of lips
that moves out
beyond the darkness,
and a rose
kisses the space
of lovers
eyes
the tender
glove of thought
sharpens the
blades of
instant growth.


1/19/76




**WILTED FLOWERS**

Please tell me of tell the twist
that it takes to crawl through the world,
when your hands and feet are gone.
And also the wind that sees itself
in the pillows of dream,
folded up in the lost passion
of wilted flowers.


1/19/76

**BREEZE**

The breeze
       is
                the
                              passive touch
            of the eye
                  looking backward
  in the
       b
        l
         e
         e
        d
        i
         n
        g
                moment.

1/20/76


**THE PLACES IN THE PLASMA DAWN**

The places in the plasma dawn,
where the old eagles
and tears
of their torment,
are the excited
moment in the eye
of your material cloud.
Your dawn has stripped
its eagle
and leaves it
daring to run with
the naked crowd.

1/20/76

*1976*

**BLUE DUST**

The blue dust
of the hemisphere
the talking dizzy
clasp of the hand
where the rose
touches the eyeball
on the wind
my tongue
is the flame
of the wind
I cry sweet melodies
to the saxophone smile
that touches me
where the moonlight
whistles to the moon


1/23/76




**IN THE MORNING**

At the bottom of the sea,
at the bottle of a glass
peering into the sky illusions
of my heart
a bird takes flight as morning blooms
in my hand
and I run into the wind
with my feet
touching the cosmic clouds of tomorrow dreaming
like the spaceships of the eye
that cross the wind with my
speared tongue.


1/23/76

## SPEAR INTO TOMORROW

There are ripe bowls in your face like drops of honey
on your beard that is lace, that is an angry smile of patient love.
The balls of fish lay their own eggs in the freshwater of their stagnant
lagoons.
I peel off the rubber mask of the villains of taste, who call themselves
the bourgeois romance
and their flies yearn to the plastic heaves of a tongue of gold and fire.
Walk backward with your face aflame and your soul touches the rivers
of tomorrow.


1/25/76




## SUN MOON

Into the direction
of the sun moon on a golden spike called my tongue
with silver fingers and an eye for the lost corners of a jade bull that
bounces
off into the haze of my dreaming minstrels of joy, that is where my
voice speaks in hunger for the words
of flame


1/25/76

*1976*

## TICKER TAPE ILLUSIONS

Ticker tape illusions
that swallow the dawn
on rosebud happiness
of folded sparrows.
The knife licks
the bleed temple
of gratification
the monument of jade
is the face
of the hungry
crowd that wanders
aimlessly
and afraid of the wolves
that parade
wearing plastic masks
and woolen covers
to hide their shame

1/26/76

## LET ME TALK TO YOUR ROBOTS

Let me talk to your robots
who always resemble dogs
in heat.
Let me speak to the
rubber tongues
of fly madmen
with cow wallets
and flesh brains
that moo in the night.
Let me assemble
the night with my fingers,
arrange the clouds
beneath my swollen touch
then I will open
the staircase
of its worth
and empty the drawers
of their flesh clothing
at that time I will
be beyond my ice
and be free to strike
anywhere I choose.


1/28/76

*1976*

**MY CRITICS HAVE PUT ME TO DEATH**
**(for Federico García Lorca)**

My critics have put me to death,
their eyes rain sadness
because they knew me
all too well,
their lips cried apologies
and they wept their sorrows
and fired their guns,
they spoke with no one
of my assassination
and only praised my life
in darkened rooms.

I have spoken words,
a thousand, thousand years
and pierced
a thousand, thousand ears
that ran to hide
or stayed
to weep with me
under the sun.

My critics have put me to death
and they knew my name
and knew my fire,
for they held the water
to douse the flames,
but failed to see
the embers that rolled
to meet the dry grass
of burning desire.

My critics have put me to death
and hid my body away
in the volumes they
thought they burned,
but my tongue
still licks the air
with the fury of remembrance,
with all their fears
of my longing return.
My critics have put me to death

with their bullets and ignorance,
with their injustice,
and their blindness.
My critics have put me to death,
and in doing so,
have also executed themselves.

1/28/76

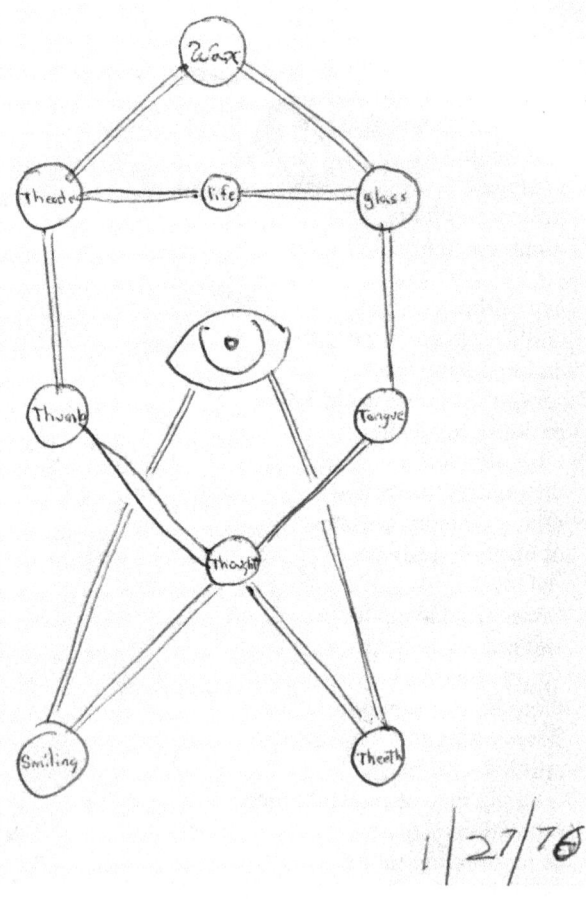

*1976*

**SPEAKING TO THUNDER**

The ivory gods
of Asgard speak
to me out of leadened mouths
and lick all the phosphorous
honey from my lips
we talk together
in the haze of our longing
where the moon dies
in the bleeding night
the open cell
on the dreams
of ancient crosses
ah, I feel stripped of a cane of sugar
and swallowed whole in the anger
of feeding nations that drawl


1/28/76




**GAP TOOTH**

The space in teeth
       ok,
the room at the end of drawers
where an eye seeks
the solutions
of a stale breakfast
the tabletop
shines with polystyrene shine
and blood lickings
of the rose
turned backward
in your eye


1/29/76

## WEDDING OF BLOOD

The blood of your wedding
is an open door into eyes of longing
I space into your living room
where your T.V. screams madness at me
and I roll on the carpet of glass dreams
eating the spaces in the clouds that are birds.
With tears woven into your blanket
with fine threads and stolen hearts
the beasts that lurk in the shadows of fear,
disrobes before your dirty eyes
The ivory passersby under the moon of madness
possess the dream of green leaves that burn in your eyes.

1/29/76

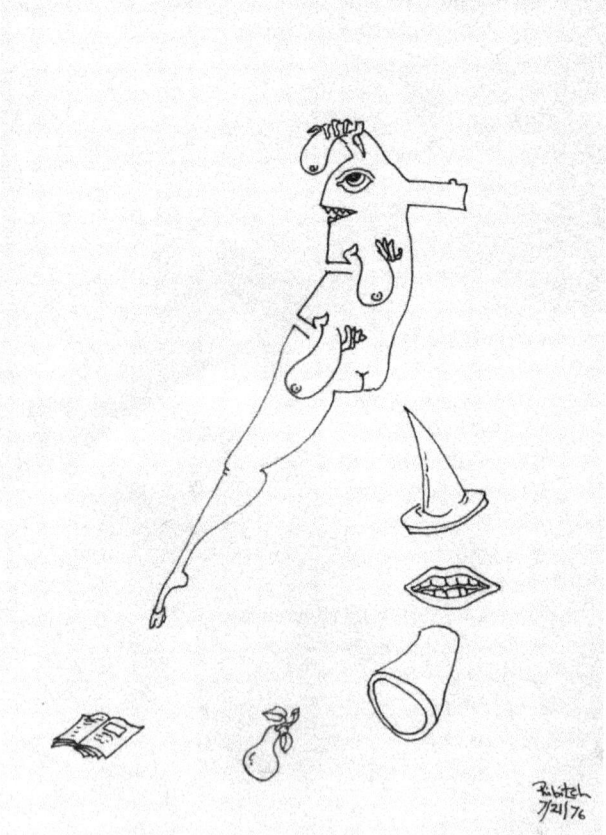

*1976*

**BIRD HANDS**

I bent my hand into a bird
and felt the tears
of cracked time fill
my space
with my tongue
there are quarters
that bleed the eagle wings
in the air of the fire
my eyes are whales
migrating in death
past the bus stops
of their sorrow
the clock cries
the sweet wheat breath
on the wind
and swells its ankles
with broken blood
and turkeys
cut their wings
with rusty saws
for their flight
is stunted in
their sorrow


1/31/1976


**COSMIC SPACE**

The cosmic space of fiery eyelids
the tongue of Isis on the throne of Ibis
The pyramid of stone eyes walks backward
into the conclave of walking feet.
Into the jumbled mannequin's eyes
my soul who is owl-hunting
with golden fingers for the dogs of Sirius


1/31/76

## I AM A BLEEDING RHINOCEROS

I am a bleeding rhinoceros
with hands of gold.
My eyes of bleeding wood
Pulled from the fires of the extinguished.
Knighthood's flight
into the spacious tongue
of slit throats
speaks to the hexagrams
of my mouth.
The eyes of my youth
run backward
into the sun,
and into the caustic dream
of angelic lips
that are parted and set aflame
in the fecal movement
of moments slipping
away beneath my
protruding forehead
that can only
be speaking to the frogs
of the sun
that set fire
to my soul.


1/31/76

*1976*

## INTERFACING INTO THE BLEEDING MOON

Interfacing into the bleeding moon
of my hand, into the soft memory
of scalded romance and robots of deep caves,
that swims with their eyes into
the total space of bleeding love and wounded hatred

For the repeating eye
and the total amount of the tongues
that goes past the ears
of no hearing and into
the space of rusted blood.


1/31/76




## DEAD SOIL

I dive into the dead soil of longing,
of swimming into the belief
of long tongues and fire night.
The muzzle death of the gun.

And the noose of tongues that penetrate
into the caverns of time
let those tears fall away into the slobbering eye of the sun.


2/1/76

## MY EYE

The lips of my eye
fly into the cosmic
star of hallucinated dream
to fish the memory
of fire romance
from the pools
of desire's flesh
the whole cake
of long intent
under the moon
that is crystal
and blazing
with desire's scream
with the whole illusions
of the sun,
and the sun
screams at the eye
of my spirit.

2/1/76

*1976*

**SPAIN**

Where the Boon
takes its fingers
to kiss the stars
of their loving embers
to flame
under the Spanish noon
to touch the
Spanish landscape
my tongue
tastes the wine
of my eye
and loves
the soft silk
touch of the flame.

2/1/76

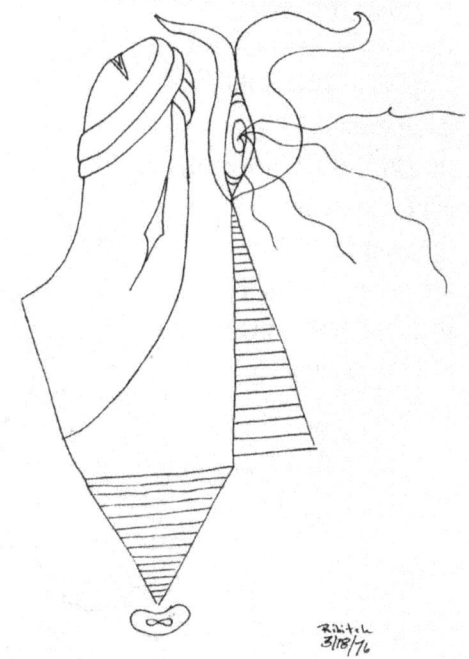

## TRANSPORTED HUNGER

Transpose the hungry women
of desire's cut throat,
enter the mouth
of a longing touch
the hemming bird of fire
who distinguishes itself from rice
or the distillery of bad taste.
Romance with the bargain basement
of desire's organ.
We leave on a boat to Spain,
and enter the lagoons of
startled carnivals,
where clowns bow
their heads
in plastic reverence
to thunder and lace.
Appeal to stretching
a hand out and into
the dust of the horizon.
Many discussed eyelids
that run from them
knowing that the river
of blood tastes the tongue
of their desire.

2/1/76

*1976*

**FEVER**

Envisioned fire
takes your tooth
by the eye
and twists
the body-jerk
of thunderous
nose bleeds
the well
of bleeding wallets
protruding tongues
of screaming
rictus
the knife
filters
into the stomach
wall of
amorphous
coffee stains.


2/2/76

## THE STAR

The star
       is
flaming
       the
          moon
              dance
seeking
       out
       the
       sun
        m
        a
        s
        t
        e
        r
                of liberated
                     sorrow

2/2/76

*1976*

**A ROOM OF SUFFERED FISH**

The monotony of your fist
bleeds in the boredom blue
of a distinguished flame,
that of an owl's bleeding,
that of the stale taste
of blood wine.
The long wait in scalded rooms
with pants without pockets
and eyes that lead
into mirrors of cracks.
A woman enters carrying
a bowl of water,
she severs the tops
from flowers
and sings to the goldfish,
songs of stale harmonies
and reminiscent longings.


2/3/76

**BLOOD MOON**

Blood moon
like the dog at the bottom
of the broken bottle
of silver dreams.
The stake of eyelids
tears the tallow
of dream
in the seed of trash.
The breaking book
of judgment
is falsifying the fact
of green bush attacks.
The screen, the bubbles
of love are breaking
the split wrist
of eyes laughing.


2/3/76

*1976*

**DECAPITATION**

There stands the blood feast of a thousand years.
Marble caskets cover the tombs.
The yellow bleeding flowers that wail their sorrows
to the dying multitudes, who wait in the hungry
mouth of the lion death.

The stone of letters are etched out in the wind.
The sorrowful screams of ravens that dance
and the ribbons of their birth test their place
at the bottom of pits and at the bottom of alleys.
In cold blood the clocks arrange the angle of the wall.

The pictures that lean into the faces of counted
disbelief and wonder fall into the cracks in the floor,
lay cryptograms to the faceless eyes that search every corner
to steal a touch of the cutting crystal that bleeds the suicidal.

The shrink crosses out the lines of thinking
His madness swallows whole the fears of nations that bleed
like beheaded birds.

2/3/76

**FLIGHT OF DEATH**

The lick of the fevered moon
eats all the rabbit bastards
of the red soil
and broken feet.
The monster magnet of the sun
runs madly backward.
The silver wristwatch
of my face runs naked with buzzards.
The nickel-plated blasts
exterminate my lips
that are on fire.
Weeds bleed
for the angles of desire.
I wander in the fog
and wear leggings
made of iron and rust.
The faceplates are broken
and they cannot see
the forests that are
burning in tears.


2/5/76

*1976*

**GAGGED**

Spiral spittle
looking into the eye
of gold misfortune,
the lack-eyed dogs
of blue venues,
the central brain attack,
of heart seizures.
Their hearts are stripped
of plastic size-o-graphs.
The bleeding wounds
of daylight are looking
into the empty mind
of the intellectual beast
that carries their brains
in brown bags
to explode later
in the empty rooms
of wasted memory.


2/5/76

## ESCAPING FROM THE BEAST

Escaping from the beast
on the eyes of an
executed Judas,
his finger swollen,
his eyes twist backward,
and sight fought
through the rose,
that rose bleeds
in the morning frost,
the blood softening
the hands
of crying clowns,
who pass out
in the rain,
that time
is the moment
of the freezing dawn
that wilts
like fingers
of dead poets.


2/6/76

*1976*

**SPASTIC TIGER**

Spastic tiger,
the leaves of fire
and the ducks of memory
run into elevators
of convulsive time.
The elevator operators
are naked,
stretching their penises
to the third floor
of madness...
The ducks run away
from themselves,
their eyes following
in mad laughter.
The cold turkeys
wear horns
and leather zippers,
to step out of
their breasts and faces.
The coffins of enormous
dreams make faces
in mirrors of cracked,
and burned madness.
The birds of
grinning love,
open the chest
to squeeze the clock
of convulsive living.
Plastic drawers
contain the rubber eyes
of now and then.
Look into the empty
look of a poets eyes.

2/6/76

**MY SKIN HAS TURNED TIGHT**

My skin has turned tight.
I can no longer bear its existence.
My throat constricts
where my voice is strange
and distant in the smoke.
My eyes bulge.
I believe it is time
to take leave from my bones.
To take leave from this tightening skin,
from this glass-eyed wilderness.
I talk not of a suicidal
compromise with death glare,
but a leaving on
the back of a golden swan
whose back has been carved
to fit my image,
not my body,
but a resemblance
of a ghost who is a train.


12/7/76

*1976*

## ON THE QUEST OF A FLAME

on the quest of a flame
that has been taken
from the sun's
aching side
that was left bleeding
sore the wound
of swollen eyes
walking up the steps
of frozen heart
and seeing past
the rubber face
of plastic clowns
the evasive touch
of tongues running
into the faceless moon
of your time
your fat swallows
of time eat out
off the terrine
with the full baboons
whose lips are still
bloody of fresh kill.


2/7/76

## SHIP OF CRACKED GLASS

The hollow beast bellows. Turning themselves outward for a time to burn the green leaves of their yearning years away from the dying frost. They seize the power of their eyes. Walking backward and bleed the swallow tail. The blood of tired worms. The tires are bald of their worth, of their coins running madly insane, into the mirror of laughter. Caught by the face which was rubber, and stretching like lips of disuse. Their candy motives show the naked movements and vibrations of shallowness. Tall buildings made of glass and skin. There is a concrete block that resembles the faces of hunger. There are wooden ships of sorrow flying in the pale wind, to strip the sea of worth, in that they swim alone on the foam of the sea.

2/7/76

## ABSENT FEELERS

Peelers at dawn
Breakfast of riches
Envelope whole trains
Bleeding wakeups thrust
The whole bacon shop
Narcissist words open eyes
The drop of whistle screams
An angel's warning
Stop at the corner of dreaming
Spastic fingers cut open suns
Interceding of joints walk
The envelope is empty
Letters are on fire
Birds grope in the darkness
Inner-space the Maldororous dawn
The plastic nose of knife
Sew the shirt of loving

2/9/76

*1976*

**ACCIDENTAL FIRE**

Accidental fire
Process of multiplying moment
Piercing flesh of tongue
Wiping wipe of flame
Jealous eye of scream
Walking today of tomorrow
Wind run of goose flesh
The fire of spastic time
Swallow the throat
Cut the umbilicus
And swallow yourself
Bleeding whole
Rye and mountains
Plying insight into dream

2/10/76

## EXONERATE THE BELLOWS OF LOVE

Exonerate the bellows of love.
Set aflame the water ducts of freedom
The blue onset of madness
screams with fire eyes of love's dream
and demonstrates the swallows of desire.
Walk into doors of lips,
and kiss the walls
in absence to nothing.
The spark of a match
Opened the trellis of burning desire,
the desire beyond honor.
Love keeping time with footsteps
that open door of screeching.
Love's arms of wax swans
are naked refreshments of water.
The bleeding moment of tomorrow
and the fish of the wealth
are lovers in the dance.
The blast of beacons,
the flower of arms budding,
and the tendrils of lips
black and blue with the honor
of sweet wealth
and of sweet love's breath.


2/10/76

*1976*

**GROSSED ONSET OF CONFUSION**

Oil lamps are set aflame, and browsing through historical volumes of taste. The birds of metamorphous has their flight into the sphere of eyes' longing intent. The absent dowry of stolen wealth that flies into the orb of self-inflection. The metallic Melrose of pondering doubt sets flame to the house of raging roses, who on the run cry for moments of greed. Snow eyes of leopards, whose flight of backward swans, swim in the depth struggle with the mask of fleeing monarchs without their crowns of thorns. Rage entwine insane Cut seeds of flight Moment of blood taste The rope frayed and dropped from a plane to fall limp in the castle of flying tomorrow. The stapled chest. Magnet tongue. Open the casket ears Flask of swollen feet walking backward again into the free zone of collective cerebral explosion. Asphalt dream Dreamers motion Of movements scream And all those wine taste seem bitter in the haze of blue fog.

2/10/76

## LAUGHING BARK OF FISH

Seed of saddle flights
An ostrich of a dozen deaths
peeling back the eggshells
of continuous laughter
on the broken spell of the Magi's kiss.
The massacre of black birds
with their tongues sealed
in the ointment of disbelief,
open their tongues that walk in the park.
The managers of disappointment
squander away the ropes
of hanging convicts.
Their blood is open to criticism.
Their life is open to doubt.
Blood leaves the mountains
of their sorrow.
Break open jars of pabulum
Feed the hungry bears of problem.
The pools are full of semen
The cold sperm jealous
for the monster cities.


2/10/76

*1976*

**LEOPARD'S DANCE**

Crashing eyes thundering
The split wrist of running
Cabinet of grace splitting
Mountain of space
After the moment running
Like a wail of death
Fingering the mask of torn faces
Ruling the paper of dawn burning
That space of tears
Broken records of time
Eyeing lost frail children
The bus is moving without me
Into some unseen quarter
The moon is lion
Smell of sweet sweat
Cry of slit gazelles
And running madness
Of summer's time
To bleed the soft wound
Pray an envelope
The face of plastic mirrors.


2/10/76

## BLOOD IN THE MORNING

The buds of roses

Eyes clash into tongues

The black forest

Of spayed dogs leap

The hungry wallet

Jeweled bellies

Raisin toast of blood

Sets alone on the beach

Talking to cloud birds

Hang in execution of sadness

Their fingers swollen

Eyes cut by glass

Tongues waving Badly

The air is burnt

The diamonds of eyes melt

Freedom in silk

The spastic dawn

Records the blessedness

Cross of burnt fingers.


2/17/76

*1976*

**A LEATHER APPLE YEARNING**

A plastic man was manacled
to the back of the train.
The black and blue hand covered
his face with twisted knockwurst.

The savage fist is bleeding on
a salt tongue near the haunted balcony,
where the stairs are of burnt wood
and are crumbling.

The plastic man is naked and flayed.
His skin of warm noises cover
His nose of plain wood.
His penis severed and sewn to his forehead.

The glass jaw of pelicans
are the running boards of faces,
bleeding with their tongues speaking.
The yellowed earth's skin is
broken radios for listening ears.

The last moment of glistening shouts
a razor blade fortune
of cookies broken off in the mouth.
Lips are cut and watering.
The water can nose.
Spastic quiver of fingers,
wooden and plastic are
lead and poison.
The dagger-less positions
of robot jealousies fill the room.

2/21/76

## A POLITICAL PHRASE

A promise for a new day
I lead a horse with frayed face
To a pit to throw it in
The apples bleed on the trees
A new open door extracts
Wind from head explodes
The doll frame of coats
A rescue squad of cats
Shove a fist into hairy jars
Their own breath wilts
Doors come off hinges
Linger beside stately autos
Burn the tabloids of diplomats
Their fingers caught in the cash box
Swollen and pitiful
In plight and rage
Their flag shot and burned
The gray sky of a face
That lingers on the shores
Of San Clemente


2/21/76

*1976*

**HAND OF WHITE**

My hand of white
My bird of ivory screams
The wilted finger nails
My wallet of bleeding cow
Swallows moments in glass
Screaming drops of meat
Running madly backward
My hungry face
My swollen lips talking
My feet running without me
The storm swells in haste
The broken phonographs
Label of-deception
Nose bleed
Crossing the street of romance
The eye of naked vultures
Grossing the bees of fortitude
Squeeze a cloak
My white hand in silk
My blood in a pool
Frozen with my keepers
Smiling like madness


2/21/76

*Ribitch: The Last Word, Volume 1*

**MORNING AFTER THE BOMB EXPLODED**

The hot taste of severed mannequins
Their amazing breath dying of grief
The quilt of madness
Tongue and cheek
Running after lame feet
Their crossbow
Entangled in my hair
The night licking tulips
Manacled dawn
Opening the white teeth
Of frothy fish
Angry swallow of correctness
Accidental roses cling
Madly stemming out
Where automobiles collide
Animal faces of megaton gladness
The automobile dildo
Of dreams
Fasten the elastic cord
To the endless bedroom


2/21/76

*1976*

**THE SNEAKING AXE**

The warm pudding keeps ears
The erasable notebook
Run into the fathomless depths
Of a cave rolling afterward
An earmark of worms
Dress in jeweled gowns
The mask of unseen bandits
Crawling out of television sets
Speaking to jars of wheat
An axe lay backward
Across the eyebrow of smiling
Accident freshness
A doughnut of scalded voices
The breaking point of tongues
A needle thread through
A vessel hand
Spoken tongues of penguins
Laid in embroidered sketches
The mother of laziness
Open eye of stretched puckers
Can opener on my open palm


2/21/76

**AVENUE OF BLOOD**

Roses of empty bloody faces
walking to hurried floors and platforms.
Speeches of voiceless politicians
with tankers of beer and sweat.
The flowers of stainless youth
singeing the eyelids' revolution.

Revolution of walking birds
Revolution of stolen flowers
Revolution of asking questions
Revolution of the abyss of stone

The quarry of rocks
where the blood of the executed
singing the bath of death
in the space of revolution's bleeding mouth.

Revolution of silence
Revolution of opened doors
Revolution of stretched suspenders
Revolution of dying grief
Revolution broken clocks

Send troops to Chicago.
        Revolution
Sending politician pimps to Washington
        Revolution
Sending cheeseburgers to Viet Nam
        Revolution
Sending enemas to Angola and Los Angeles
        Revolution

Revolution of played cards
Revolution of glass eyes
Revolution of manacled wrist
Revolution of burning buses

*1976*

    Death on Detroit assembly line
        Revolution
    Obituary of dreams.
        Revolution
    dollars of spastic T.V.s
        Revolution
    loaded gun of ambiguity
        Revolution

The sound of screaming women
manacled imprisoned babies
fifteen beaten in strike line
blood on the floor of Saks Fifth Avenue
open wound in the heart of America.
The beast of a thousand tongues

Revolution of gray-haired anger
Revolution of charging taxis
Revolution of blown-up freight trains
Revolution of black dreams
and feet turned back toward revolution

Open heart attack on Broadway
        Revolution
The return of the angered buffalo
        Revolution
The madness of out reached hands
        Revolution

2/22/76

**MOON PIE**

The moon as part of a hand
The unicycle embarks on a voyage
Naked relevance speaks
Truth empty vase of spring
A woman, a white bird
The tangle of fingers on the subway
The glacial face of dining
Rocks bleeding at the wrist
Their cone-shaped face
Running in a circle at the moon
A black pot of coffee
The astral face of donkeys
Swollen nose of muddy talk
The back of the hand
The moon is stagnant
Overgrown melons as eyes
There in the bleak dawn
Is the relevant twitch
Of swollen suns


2/22/76

*1976*

**PRIME TIME**

The dawn of death with leaves
A springboard vomiting
A spastic realm of walking
Red
Flying blood of politicians
White
Screening eyes of Klu Klux Klan
Blue
Drowning beneath pools of infiltration
Smiling car salesman
Looks like my grandfather's open trunk
Stripes
A prison of hope castrated
Fingers of walking judges
Stars
A field of emptiness
A mouse of lurching teeth
A house of burning wood
A cage of eyes
Fleeing after the bellows
Of an empty clock


2/22/76

*Ribitch: The Last Word, Volume 1*

**THE SENTENCE**

The leading question was
who is responsible for the murder?
A lead piece?
A frozen smile?
Did you do it in the bedroom?
Underneath pillows?

Beside the face of liars
the cross-examination of wolves,
their feet exploding,
and their noises are explanatory.

An apple of a face
Such an innocent boy.

The dagger slit the wrist of his face
In the moment of blood.
Bloody face of innocence
was the tiger's jaw.

Justice of peers
sitting on gravel stools,
bleeding beside the wall,
the wall of structure
and the stain of the execution.

2/22/76

*1976*

## A DINNER HELD FOR FOOLS

I went to bed with scandal
and the flight of my blood
walks past the dunes,
fingering rose petals.
The height of my frozen memory
is the Apple of the night.
The breaking of the wrist
wails under a tender beast of breath.
The veins of the heart
is the whole reason to dissect
the bleeding of the blood moon.
Sky of rose, father of running,
nations choking
on the blue felt of stagnant water.
Where the pool
dries up in my hand
blackness of the wound
cuts the throat of gazelles.
Their angry cries
bleat out in the saddened night
of memory.
Shot full of holes
the navel of my belly
is the lock of the wind.
The last corner of breath
where the people gather
to roast a dead goose
the death the tribute of daylight.

2/27/76

## POET IN THE MIRROR OF DOUBT

The rivers of bloodless night. The olive branch smell of arms on the blade of dream. Touch the often sometimes scream of gripping blades. Diamonds of milk. The death of madness. Walking with the eagle of dreams. Suns of tormented beds. The afterthought of daydreams. The night's swift death of raving fingers. The often smelt wallet of dream. The wild roaming grunt. After taste. Madness, madness. Enter into the soft shells of tender hate. Ask the blind men the directions to the wall. The wall of the executed. The bleeding death of their desire runs into naked disbelief. The droning flame of blackened night. The wholeness of a crazed mind. The omelet of desire's fingers bleed raging desire from a box. The mirror of melted ivory. The reflection of dawn is askew in the wind. The fingers of rubber faces. After glass beads, memory is broken on the running board. Filth of grey dust on a dozen convulsive dreams. The fires breathe of torments' remembrances. The black fire truck. Counting backward health and looking into inside-out. Spastic eyes twitch forward. The grain of the fingers and those unholy erections are the windows on the soul. The only word is to tell the truth.

2/27/76

*1976*

**SONG OF DEATH**

The ambiguous thought
Amberzille dying
The African night
Haunting of a moment's daylight
The noises that haunt me
Creep into the wall
Tiny touching fingers
The ape of sorrowful vengeance
Carrying a basket of death
The robot chains of prison
Death wrapped in brown paper
Death in the middle of a storm
Death the cattle cell of sermon
Death the last name of daylight
The afterthought of miscarriage
Blanket over the eyes
Eyes death of madness
Death of dream
The rounding pit of false eyelash
Sit alone on the head of a pin
Seeking a spasm of rigor mortis
That death speaks out of tongue
The night of blame
The cut sword
Ambiguous bleeding heart
That is nailed to the wall
Of mortuary detested
The classical bud of dying
In the cheeks of wailing
The blackness of rotted eyelids
Death gong to a dance
A waltz of corporas
That sings ancient Mayan songs
Open mouth that breathes
The stale wind of blood
The talking lion of death
Death, an open wound
Death, the glassed-over eye
Death, the dance under the moon
The moon bathed in blood soil
Ask for the price of wealth
Notations on the back of skin

Dance fevered sun in dying
The box of souls buried
Death, death, death
Sing another dance
For the crying wind

2/27/76

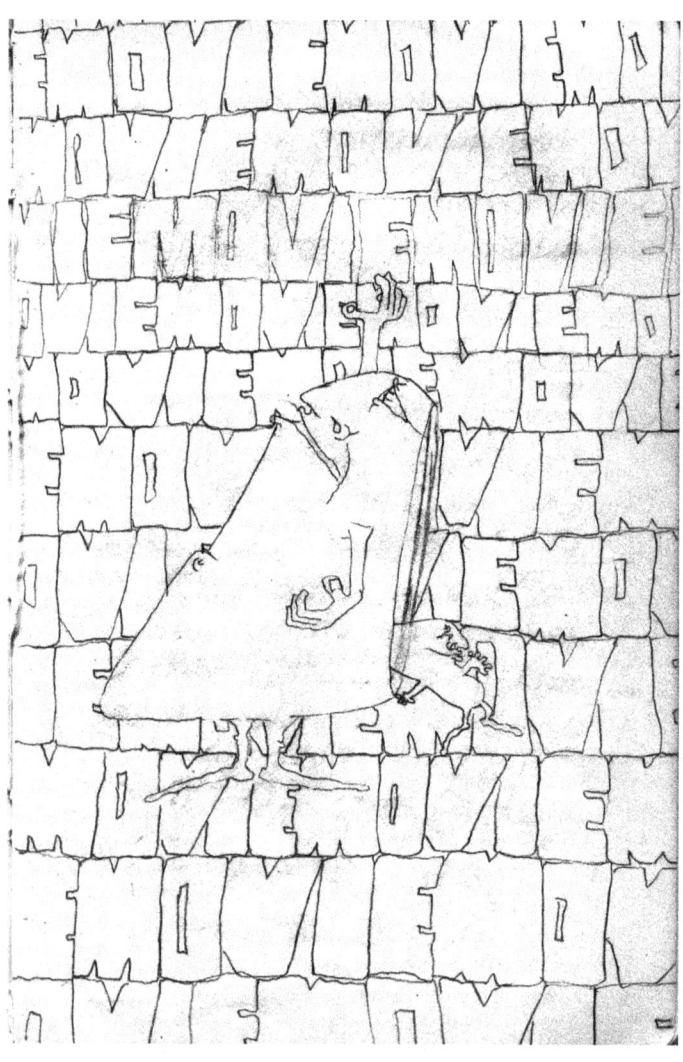

*1976*

## THE GRACEFUL HUNGER

The onset of blood
On the tireless night
      Mood dream
Past the driver's seat
The conqueror runner
With zany eyeglasses
Runs over the dead cats
See the blue hummingbird
Eat the raisin eye
Black and blue blood
Black and blue zero
      Moment of the horizon
An apple of seeds
Zebra of light
The clash of stone
The running obelisk
      Apple dome
      White death
      Powder of fault
Gleaming the thunderous auto
The green eye of spasm
The anemone of poison
Swallows itself in the dawn
While dawn thunders
Clashing the heaven's death
      In blue
In the vein of the heart
The asking moment
Of running eyes
      Dog blood
Of the sidewalk
The open flask
The open hand

2/27/76

**UNMASKED FORTUNE**

Over the crossing to the bleeding moon, the over ambidextrous watch the crucifixion of the lepers. The water of his hands is bleeding out of the wound. The mask of his feet is stretching out maddened palms to the sky, with the torment of a beggar's song. The evening's blackness is the vile vomit of the wrist. The asking multitude of correctness, open the door to the grave. Let loose the demons of fire, and their drapes of golden flask their sheep's head romance. The dungeon of screams is the frog's dance, playing lightly into the eye of death's palm. Suicide of the eagle covered the freshness of the dawn. Open your mouth swollen bleeder, hemophiliac of tongue. Carry out the beaches of jade aphrodisiac.

> Look at yourself.
> You're older, hung by the neck.

Your face lingers awhile with the spacious dust of blood. Walk with the wise-men of death. The sorrows of your youth gleam like the jade asphalt of tears and this is your epitaph.

2/28/76

*1976*

**SPITAL BROKEN JAR**

The seat is empty and broken
Train seat asphalt
Gross inset foot nail
Lingering post of lightning
Scrape boot basil rift
Cat's elbow rowing croft
Ladle spit
Iron drone bowl rafter
Nickel-plated angle spare
Ass buckle broom switch
Nose red thorn grower
Bedding bye open door
The day of little orphans
Sweating molting ribbon fry
Glass seed nothing bit
Hagel rot funny gut
Spin cradle pot
Bird feather eye spot
That's needle baby's blood


2/29/76

## WALK ABOUT THE TREE NAIL

Rowboat sprain wobble
Snake pit run dice aftermath
Roman affiliate
Showers of relief
Scrabble heir toothache
Run across the wire
Pools fold foot parade
Nickel shines never more
Pay toilet open door
Room empty crossbow
Bird of fly speckle
Roar plane
Cackle laugh nose cross
Spade of ace
Explosion roar foot paddle
Naked jubilance
Hair bleed callous
Phone of phonic jealousies
Suspended bridge
Capillaries bursting bubble
Mirror face looking back
Awl's lip torn inside-out
The trio's done
Over now


2/29/76

*1976*

**A HOLE IN THE HEAD LEAKING**

The black sparrow is nailed to crossbones
Like ingested shallowness of blinding knighthood
St. Anthony, with his cross of rose-blood fire
and the Jewess of bleeding remembrances,
they each hack and howl in the jackal weeds.
Through the glass harp runs
subliminal blowers of frost cones.
The magic finger of running,
asks the bone-white stone laughter
to cut the skin open, widely censoring
the maniacal disbelief of forgotten chains.
The seeds luster, like a bone bruise
is looking for a scent,
the smell of rubber and alabaster.
Broken needles and the seamstresses thread.
The token maiden and her madness
The bird of cranial bliss
have asphalt tires that are blown apart.
Death is three times everything.
The Masterful glint of dust
on those breaking glass splinters.
Past the bakery shop windows
the last one standing is draped in lace seeking
the whole multitude of gross mistakes.

3/1/76

## JUNKET RUN FLUX

nail to the bleeding wall
an axe to execute timelessness
fake face of bubbling
frozen fire standing
the ant's notation of amberzille
orchid of smiles
after fixing roses' laughter
the only maid slaughter
cream executed wall to wall
taxi of rotten meat
lobes of ears aftermath
the reel of film
tiny broken seeking long
the face of level ptomaine
junket run flux


3/1/76


## DROPLET OF SKY

the droplet of sky
angles it's right
into the darkness
of foaming space
of the laughing dawn
the nickel of sun
eye of clinging
a load of sap


3/3/76

*1976*

**BLACKEST MOMENT**

The blackest moment of secret mud
flung into the faces of passing giants,
who call out the guard of their hammers.
The naked atolls of castrated humor.
The bars leveled at the chest.
The cranial resemblance of feces
looking into the rouge heavens
of multicolored glass statues,
that parade past the swallows
of their own respite.
Gondolas sink in the canals,
after filling up with fecal piles.
The city management fish for dollars,
along the Nile of their dreams.
Wooly mammoths still live
on 182nd St.
swallowing whole acorns, alive.
Running with big feet,
and crushing all that is stepped on,
pudding is cheaper that way.


3/4/76

## CRANIAL KISS OF DEATH

The lazy dolls of her arms take from
        the earth parasols of fish.
The elastic scream of madness to touch
        her suicide with searching fingers.
The face of her eyes ran into the darkness
        to play with the pest.
Open door on the forgotten lullabies sings
        the sweet mood of molded tears.
Glass broken, she wanders over her baked flesh
        to the white death of the sun.
The nakedness of strewn flowers allows for
        the midnight to take peeks.
The flimsy open window of an empty room
        waits the dawn for warmth.
She sits in a chair and waits for the
        hungry taste of running life.
The black gun she held in her hand smiled
        and guessed her fate.
The rose wilted in a jar next to scrabbled
        words that came over the radio.
The chill of an evening dress cut open
        at the neck speaking.
The frail moment of fright that had
        an open hand on death.
A glint-eyed negress of the last swinging
        light overhead heard words.
The radio spoke sweet whispers into the
        lonely ears failing to grasp.
Angel of whiteness, sweet death on a pillow
        stained with workers' blood.
Half with hope, taking the dung of need
        and kicking back on an overdose.
The spasms of love courted the disbelief
        of a spaniel's cry.
And alone in triumph, the winning glance
        into the mirror full of creeks.
Her hands aged in a single night what
        seemed to be centuries.
The mask of worn-out fear came to close
        and strangled forgotten smiles.
It was too late as the cock crowed beneath
        the billows of illusion.

*1976*

She lay swollen in her death, eyes
        piercing the ceiling.
The wail of the rescue-squad coming to send
        no life into her bleached body.
The night sends signals into the air that
        only the mysterious can read.
And this lip that touched none for so many
        years bled alone under dampness.

3/4/76


**EYE GLASS**

Eyeglass popping from my right hand
The tulip jade dawn
Grossed feeling of moment
After the thought of nothing
My mouth says words obliquely
A letter of letter
Swollen paper frequent misjudgments
Quality of format
Revolution speaking
Prom the headless voices of walking
They speak tantalizing tongues
From rose lips
On the staircase of ambivalence
That road to the absolute
Tarnished with nickels and bears
A brain of bleeding
Bombshell of crying relief
Stands naked and erect on the avenues


3/4/76

**PLACID CRY**

From the flower bud steam
Naked iron firefly screams
Latent dust oval rectum
Potent laser frost
Plight of moment
Laying down with birds
Intercourse of bees
Poem internal songs
Glassiness rose climb
The hovering dover
The rocks as planets
The sighing song of fortune
That tastes
A walnut world
Plaster booty's
Of oval wandering face

3/4/76

*1976*

**THE CROWNING OF YEARNING**

The great ghost of dust combs
It's hair with a comb of fish bones.
A blackened spell pierced
on the fire of barbed-wire flames.
The laughing, drowning dwarf jumps
Into the moat to sink.
A dog plays violin,
The Waltz of Grand Suicide.
On a flowing parasol.
gleaming mirrors hold off the faces
of piercing wonder.
The hatchet lady dresses
in blood and ashes.
The walking forest of Catholic priest
sit with naked women.
All of their eyes are sewn shut with
broken needles and black thread.
The apron of some dignified romance
is soiled with the cookery of fire.
Poison petals of flowers
on the cheeks of faces tender death in rows.
The lake being drained for other purposes
smells of fleeing fish.
The face of nakedness follows the whale
to the treating ground.
Unexploded bombs
fail to ignite under my hand.
While the priest sitting lonely under
Brazil trees strips his frock.
The eyelet of buttons peers as a
telescope to the unfettered wind.

3/4/76

## PRISON FLOOR

Glass eyes protruding fiery moment at dusk. The ribbon of flesh sees the smile of cinders of the virginal cross piece open on the range of doubt. See the last seagull leap to death in caverns. The swimming smell of lassoed grief surmounts the delicious mountain of green pills. Green under the haze of the moon's phosphorescent glimmerings of jade. The death of the prison guards alone, speaks with hidden pleasures that walk alone in the hunger of walls. Their own quilt is quilted in the dead flowers of madness and spoken with coins that lie upon the eyes, so that it looks inward to itself to discover the black hole of lips.

3/11/76


## SWIFT WARRIOR

Swift warrior in a plastic vest
Eating away the spattered walls.
The jeans of a dozen flies
Open death of a spilled heart
The wound of ambiguity swallowing
Naked in truth and madness
Where fingers touch
The velvet crazy of a room
That seedless death
Of a dozen romantics
Walls of sewn flesh scream
Moments of dire flash screams
To the mounds of daily run
The open door is closed
The wallet of face stolen
The beaker of romance clashed

3/11/76

*1976*

**TORN WASTE BASKET**

   A taste of frozen omelets from out of the sky. The angel of burnt feet, black like an open wound. Place of the waning a fool is set on fire. In the pit of a smile, the look of faint rose petal crashes a car into left-behind pajamas. The nose is torn free from the face, searching the over-potent jealousies with warm the air. Their overspent conduction of wires connects their backs to be warmed by naked fire. Their troubles are fine-tuned into a fish making believe its throat is covered with swift eyes.

3/11/76


**BIRD**

   The black star kisses the frail bird of desire
   Naked branch overhangs the lucid eye
   Count of blood swollen cry of tears
   The latent rumbling of forest
   The cry of tormented horse
   Cross-eyed violence of age coming
   The eye bled into the oppressive cross
   Nosebleeds of swollen moment
   Bun into a class of robots
   Disappearance into the walls
   Brick face to the agile fire
   Smith of iron twisting locks
   Ok rupture of smiles

3/17/76

**POET ON THE RUN**

Rigor mortis has set in the dead poet's hand
The leas of madness slay the untamed bark
Pouring through the wound of the throat
A black aspirin of carbolic utterings
The thick mustache caught in the blades
The poet's legs caught in the act of running
All there is to give, has been collected
The basket of pure fruit is rancid
The hallway into the dark is full of cobwebs
The poet sits and cries gray whales
The last hand of his wandering moment
Past steles and forgotten beaches
The rows of empty rifles seeking vengeance
Faces of remembered outlaws
Their only link to freedom is through mirrors
Broken, cracked, the images of paper
Burning beneath the ashes of crosses
Over burdening the labels of doorways
Left open the cattle wander with precision
Open eyes tongues drooping
Wandered legs sawed and hammered
The poet leaps to a new sun
Finds it extinguished


3/24/76




**BLACK BIRD**

Back from the sky of black bird
A leave of regret foaming
Crows of iron slow in the dust
A black hat on the head of a pin
Plowing with rusted candles


3/22/76

*1976*

## OWL OF LAKES

Are you perfect
sitting in the jowls
of a tiger's splendor?
There is a clean
break in the wall
of their breath
and sad fortune.
The tear on the paper
seeks a lonely beach
to break into a run
that rips the seams
of a flowered dress


3/22/76




## OWLS

The owls are playful fish
with diamond rings.
The suffix of talk running
into flight night.
Dogs wear tapirs of hawks
their breath of whales,
their feelers of blade
Legs wander grouping the smile


3/22/76

## THE ZEBRA THAT FANS HIMSELF

The zebra that fans himself
        sits in chairs of brick,
                his whiskers flaming,
his smile the root of the glass jar of scented fire.
Manacles of oppression that clean the face of dolls,
        their rubber masks are peeled
                flypaper injection
The toes of runners have no nails
Plastic waves and apple bullets,
the flight of raving birds and tinctures
of iodine in the eyes
Melted lips
        and the crazy cheeks of robots


3/22/76


## TIME

The mediocre rumblings of time stretch
        across the teeth of smiles.
The clocks were striped clean of their flesh
        and false values.
They know nothing of wax lips changing shape
        and position before the walls.
Time ripped from the chest of clocks
        who is nothing but themselves.
They are tied in knots every twelve inches
        and lit with cold flame.
Snake bit on the floor with a wrist watch
        at the floor of yearning.
That is a smile that was never brought
        forth in a bag of time.
Ticks and tocks are senile in the
        fresh dawn.
They are rusted with sad metal and old time.


3/22/76

*1976*

**WALKING ROBUST**

Anonymous walking of rabid rabbits
Fleeing on haunches of silver
The wax face of leopards
The rock smile of lunch
Crossing the street of hungry wasp
Naked screaming pebbled roses
The eye talks to the wells
The naked corpse flew into split vines
Rock pile tongue loafing crosswinds
The tired robot is eager
Their gross monies fall plain
Their smile is frozen peas
Flipped anger of walled holes
The sleet of crow sees itself walking
The timesheet was open to the wind
The breakfast of lips running


3/22/76

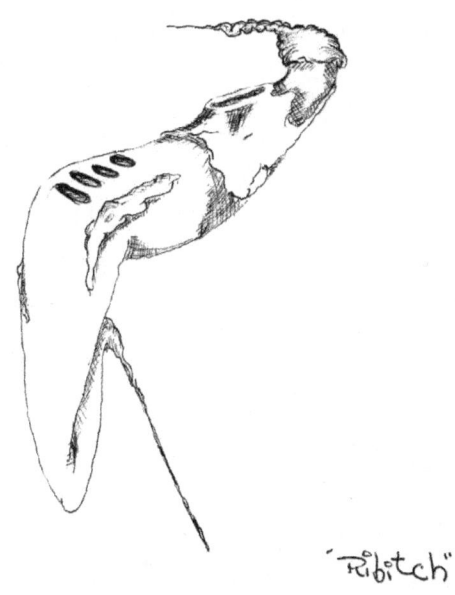

## FAILED HEART

Mastering black butterflies,
who steal reaches into the spring.
False lead openers
of the face in the mirror.
Envelopes are opened,
and the breathing looks in.
Talk of craziness…
The lip of golden earrings
and the swan of plastic conjecture.
walk with the wakeful in the breeze
of tenuous time.
There beyond the clocks that are burning,
the black swan with crab feet
is eating the stars.
No sky to touch with the hand.
No river to run backward.
Seeing that it is all torn,
that the angel of boars
rips her own heart out.
That the glass partition
is only an illusion.


3/24/76

*1976*

**AMORPHOUS PLIGHT**

Amorphous flight, the horse's tickled
face opens the breath of a walrus
The split tooth of cranial ice
The apple throat split into the sea
The elephant rage continuous old
radios hum
the plastic dawn of feathers
the ice cycles of crawling moment
blade of fuming grass talks
the broken touch on the table
glass breaks bottles of iodine
into a thousand blows
the frail lips move in-between
the open roof of flame


3/25/76

## CROSSBOWS OF METAL YEARNING

Faceless runners of stone
counting the quarters of broken legs.
Plaster faced and cracked,
the elephants of madness
their groins split,
and their only legs bent.
A face of crow was following
A monstrous cat with jaws
snapped about the arms of statues.
Their wilted necks weep
in the apex of time.
Open mouth on leprous glass
in the space where wires crossed.
The needle of fresh doubt
is an open glass mouth about to speak.
A horse of lame touch
bent into crazy relief
of dormant gray spiderwebs of shoes.
Shoes with feet of sparrows.
The partition across the floor
with the peek hole into mysterious lakes
and the cave with no one in it.
A flask of cow stomach was bursting
open the chest of diamond horses.
Their flesh crisp under the moon
bent nails over the coffin lid.
If it's a question of naked lovers
a broken nose, a broken runner
or the flayed wire birds of existence,
that is the moment of tired crosses,
that speaks to metal angels in the forest.


3/26/76

*1976*

**EYELID**

On the run there is nothing left to look at
There are glass jars above the window
There are no fake memories of lust
Cranial beat hood where no bird flies
The lost horse of grass
Feet flee from the broken clubs of wilted sky
There is a bloody hamlet on the rooftops
The plastic cover of walls
There are no wild jackets in the wind
There are no burned oats to feed dead horses
Black wrist slit for favored luck
Their only relief of somnambulant baskets
Baskets of empty confusion
Their hearts bleed fiery wreaths
Burn down the chapel of lonely regret
Their wild birds claw the wind
Their beaks sing songs silent in the brush
Only out in the rocks bleed the wind
With feet of rubber glaze the stars crow
With filth in spirit the blackbird roost
The lacking moment of poets running


3/26/76

**LAST MOMENTS**

There in the last moments
of quelling breath.
Doors are wide open seeking
to conclude justice.
That face of wandering.
The open tooth in the mouth.
Smile at what is left of nothing.
Half-forgotten faces.
Screams of night softness.
The angel hair of regret.
The walls of bleakest romance
The running backward.
Ply into the stream.


3/28/76




**LAST MOMENTS**

There in the last moments
of quelling breath
doors are wide-open seeking
to conclude justice.
That face of wandering
is the open tooth in the mouth.
Smile at what is left of nothing.
Half-forgotten faces
screams in the night's softness.
The angel of the hairs of regret,
sits upon the walls of the bleakest romance,
then running backward
it plays into the stream.


3/28/76

*1976*

**LOCKED AGGRAVATION**

Voyage into the ageless dark,
Into the pitiless mouth
whose tongue was glass
and cracked panes.
The women who wore a green velvet gown
burned and forgotten
eye the horse of burden, which walks a crazy path
with lepers and thieves,
Wine and cheese,
the milk fist of lost desire
wounded in battle or chained
to looking into every person of lead,
poisoning beats the wind with
labeled fist


3/28/76




**MAGIC**

Wandering bird
        youth deep chasms
        of charming flight
the bird of glass
the green dust of songs
        bleak sun
the fragment of slight rust
        frozen in indelible ink
        like the bust of black
charms the witch voodoo magic
        of slipped face
their wallets scream into the night
        they like,
the rest feel the glass break in the heart.


3/28/76

## PEERING INTO CRACKS

I peer deep into the cracks in the sidewalk,
hunting for the peerless night.
My blood reaches into full sacks of the moon.
The toil of my mind meets the fullness of the night.
There on the crook of my knee lie silent,
the broods of half-grown violences,
that twist the curvature of my thoughts.
The milestone of conscious conjecture,
is bleeding on the wall of shot glances.
The statue of burnt forgivings
reaches far out into phosphorous indignity.
That moment of frail blood,
That tender lace of skin,
is roaming around the base of stone.
The glass wire constructions,
are the eyes lifted into the seemingly burning forest,
where beads of sweat lie on the face.
The expression of guilt and fashion
lie on lips' movement
and the day of the marking
holds up the fish of desire.


3/29/76

*1976*

**BLEAK CRASH**

The horse choked on silver silk threads of daylight
There was a stain on the black night
Swallowed diamonds of flesh
They look into the eyes for hope resembling a skull
Mouths that rumble foul language to the dying wind
The worm of Odessa speaks classical melodies
Madonna of radios crucified to stakes
The bloom of wilted flags
The classical sadness that stems across fields
The rubber Pincers bend violently inward
More violently crosswise
There is a field of dead people
The glass cracked faces linger
They walk on asbestos flooring
Their wallets cry leather
Folding the wind like paper
Eyeing the naked trees of breastless women
Taking the train of plastic saviors
The robot loveliness of raw lips
They can only speak to the wall of consolation


4/3/76

## LOST WORLDS

Home of the silver bleeding
        The duck of murderous content
Flight of singing spears
        Wondrous blackened spikes
Bird of milk feathers Legs of ivory and glass
        Worm wood dressers
Open mouths of canaries
        Yellow and spiteful
Running with legs aflame
Calling to the rushes, the call
        Flight where no hand ever went
White hands bloody
        Bone dry eyes tearing
The walls crumble knowingly
The scream of the blue whale
        Wanting to be loved
In that moment the sea turns transparent
        Revealing the lost worlds of Atlantis

4/4/76

*1976*

**BEYOND THE MIRROR**

Unfolding the resemblances
on polymorphic layers
of fragmented time,
the cross-beams of boned realities,
stand naked before the eyes
that have been placed
beyond the looking glass of an experience.

The backwardness of everything
that we perceive as real and concrete,
as it all changes with a polymorphic response.
Nakedness takes on a new form,
with the fullness that expands
and touches the marvelous
just beyond the waiting doors of perception.

Out into the clearing,
where chimeras of Daffy Duck
call out to you and your ears,
now being accustomed to newly heard sounds
or visions that lick your newly formed eye,
beckon you to come closer to see
what Alice had really discovered in wonderland.

4/7/76

**BROKEN GLASS AND FROZEN EYES**

    The glass broke in the hands of frozen eyes. There beyond the darkness howls the sadness of twisted clocks, their fingers flowering, their mouths searching caverns of colorless space. With my cold searching hands clasped to the ceiling, I reel about dizzily. Fragrant mist swallows the feet of the sun. Look into the ancient periods of rustic mammals. My ears are marmosets. My face, the goalless pigeons of gold. The feet of colossal beasts taken afoot past my glance. I take it all in my fist. The horses breathing becomes flagrant. The apples on the highway rot with each movement of the sun. I know from the smell of the wind that the broken records of my faith have overplayed.

4/11/76

## SOAP OPERA

The glass on the floor is scratched
The broken needle erases the grooves
The hallway that was crowded is empty
The basket is full of heads
The wall is disappearing
The fingers of beast look for an entrance
The apple of languish fruited
The raceway of time runs backwards
The children slice their fingers with ice
The growing pains of pesticides
The horse of hung throat
The wax of the moon bleeds
The open door is of glass
The pens stand empty of ink
The clock of hurried passersby, waves
The flow of the sea with sight
The naked bush set aflame in rows
The total eclipse of the sun
The grand folly of murdered hands
The jury came in with the verdict of insane
The guillotine rushed like the wind
The face looked back at the beginning


4/11/76

*1976*

**MORNING OF THE SPARROW**

The morning of the sparrow
Machine gun encased in glass
The foot of moss
Electrocuted with fine fingers
The dew of frost bitten thoughts
The elastic cross, a figuration of sight
The humming projectile of prophet suns
Pyramids of cones risking the daylight
Migrating to the center of the orbs
The fire of sentinels progressing
After fix of levitation
Into the door of wonder
Past the gates of marble
The documents of desire yet opened

4/13/76

## THE ROOM THAT WHISPERS

I hear walls whispering to the soft skin of the room,
frail haunt of elephant bellows
and the smell of African jasmine heightening the tables of diamonds.
A house full of beetles with crystal voices
and nostrils full of flamboyant voyeurs
are breaking the doors or clandestine discoveries.
The fresh footprints of large marina sets
daylight with the fever of malaria.
The fossil legs are set aflame on balconies.
The swan of crab legged desire is the
Zeus of transfiguration.
The house of dolls that sweat on
the balcony of muted desire
are the lips of gaunt automobiles.
The guards on the roof have been tortured,
their hooves sewn to the gate.
The walls bleed under the sun
and the vacant skin peels back the years.
The oval face leaks at the seams.
A bird of paleness shivers in the sand
and the room that whispers calls only
to the listeners.

4/13/76


## THE ROOM OF...

The room of bone marrow seeks the lily pads of spacious desire. The doors are open to its luscious mouth and the eyes wait inside to gratify the wind. The smile of dogmatic response reels back from glass partitions. The mouth is a cavern of waste and smells of a lake that is choked with fever. Fingers of the hand. Islands slap the soil of untainted reach. Toil of burning, where the lake sets fire to the shore. Their names are carved on faces. Torment of glass people with hammers, chasing the water to the edge of lake that is filled with sand and comments that are rusted and sealed with doubt.

4/25/76

*1976*

## CLOUDS OF AN AFTERNOON

The clouds of an afternoon lick plates
Their broken memory of gazelle games
Their eyes, tokens in the air
Blades free the spears of jelly
There is but one dream
Of death in the hands; of clocks
Their winding cries take loose fibers
Of plankton on the horizon
The fire of foods breaks the noose
The necks of hung rabbits scant
And their razors are free
To cut holes in the universe


4/28/76




## GLASS BEAM

The glass beam of lopsided glance
        The sun marked the cave
Lightning screams
      Apart
              From the lust
of aerial dust
        I know you well
            Glass lions
that speak holes in the night
        Candle of spears
The tongue of razors
And all the pleading
That is done
        is done with
              doors on the head.


4/29/76

## BASKET OF ROMAN LETTERS

The basket of roman letters
Filled in the heart of chrome
The elf with no legs is laughing,
His bestial feet set in glass
The flesh of somnambulant rose glitters
The ancient well of depth
The roulade of fish in a Rolls Royce
They clamor to beguile the room
With the softness of their rubber lips


5/14/76




## DELIVERANCE

To the time of inevitable beast
Stricken by the heart attack and fever
Overlaid by the rust of their magnets
They deliver the stones of hands
On the bellied floor of rum
They heat the juices of a room
A room that is aflame
With the bristly heat of death


5/27/76

*1976*

**WORDS**

My mouth opens and my teeth explode with such infinities that the bed sheets stand up in awe of their whiteness the paleness of T.B. sickly tumors. Words of frightful existences are words that split the air of my breath. Words that resemble dynamite and they explode from my teeth like diamonds. The broken syllables spill out of my tongue and resemble maggots. Words cry the bitter relief of centuries of death. Death at the fiery bosom of spilled blood. Death is countless like the words on a page. Death is like dreams in front of the mind. Like words, like roses with filed thorns. Death and words nailed tightly into the casket of years. Words that rust the nail of the casket and set free the wings of death that roam on the corpse of the executed who sit angrily in the bowels of hatred, waiting to take hold of the poets position at the head of the table that sits in flame and blood.

5/30/76

**MY EYES ARE GLUED INTO SOCKETS OF FLESH**

My eyes are glued into the sockets of flesh, seeing all the crabs sit beside trees of mist. Lakes of frozen water spill into my hand, fingers clutch the clouds, the tongue of breath. I walked out into the hallway of flame, my face looking in a different direction. The swelling of my limbs is unbearable. I can't walk with my feet looking like bats. The bats fly away with my legs. I see them disappear into the horizon. The horizon like my face looks on both sides of the hallway. The bats take their wings and pinch my toes.

6/4/76

**EGRET**

Go placidly back into your tent
Of shaded willows
Invent a blade of crazy eyes
Staring deep into lead stories
I knew it long ago
Peeling the growth of seeds of disillusion
Teapots fold their spirits
And speak to the room
Of horrible silence


7/9/76




**THERE IS AN AIR OF MYSTERY**

Let me count them one by one, or let me throw it away to the sharks of deprivation, and do I throw it at your foot to watch it roll needlessly off the edge of the world? Ah, maybe it too is stuck in the glass. Maybe the center of a shell is all there is to eternity, a marble lost in the shooting gallery. But do you fit in the circle of flameless stars? Your hearts not quite changed to a horse for your escape, and if you peek deep into the hole of thought there is a mirror, the mirror is painted black, leaving an air of mystery, for there can be no face behind it since your eyes became fish in the air.


7/9/76

*1976*

## POEM FOR CHARLIE PARKER (Version 1)

Hear the call of Othello's breath
as it takes flight in the wind.
The moth of a giant's song,
and there in the rushes fire takes it along
to see the magical stones,
the tones of a blessed fire,
the stones of migratory inflections.
The choirboy hustles in the dark.
The tongue sings of magnets.
The twisting lotion cancels the icy sky
making it open up to the infinite.
The universe of sound bending the reeds of saxophones.
The scream of the Yard bird like flames in the ocean.
The eyes screaming a moment of tremor.
The earth moves to the thunderous roar of pterodactyl whispers.
It is Yardbird in the wind.
Yard bird stretching out the last moments of life in a note.
It stands where the swallows meet to duel till death,
death that sweet stroke of the eyeing blade.
Wandering with fingers tied to clouds
where diamonds rust in the palm of the hand,
And Yard bird eats the wind to sing a song.


7/10/76

## POEM FOR CHARLIE PARKER
## (Version 2 - YARD BIRD for Charlie Parker)

The call of Othello's breath as it takes flight in the wind, south of a giant song, and there in the rushes fire takes it along to see the magical stones, the stones of a blessed fire, the stones of migratory inflections. The choirboy rustles in the dark. The tongue sings magnets. The twisting lotion candles the sky and makes it open up on the infinite. The universe of sound is bonding the reeds of saxophones. The scream of Yard bird is like flame on the ocean. The eyes are screaming a moment of tremor. The earth moves to the thunderous roar of pterodactyl whispers. A Yard bird sings in the wind, a yard bird stretching out the last moments of his life in a note. It stands where the swallows meet to duel till death, death that sweet stroke of the eyeing blade. Wandering with fingers tied to clouds where diamonds rust in the palm of the hand, and a Yard bird eats the wind to sing a song.

7/10/76

## A DREAM (Version 1)

I sit and visit dawn's crowning fingers that seem to take their time choking the night. The falsehood of years in the milk bottle of dreams, white dreams clouded over with memory. A dog walks past me wearing the saddle of his beloved father. It is the only son cherished by magnetic diamonds. The seal is broken in water pipes that leak from the heart. The falsification of a lie in a box meant for the dying. The year ended with the dead, for they forgot their smiles. Youth was spent looking for dreams, only from behind a black curtain. There were some ladies who wept on their sleeves and tarnished them. A breaking of the ghost of meticulous fingers poked at the stars. When dawn arrived it devoured ob. I settled myself in its stomach. It was there at the point of dawn that the birds of magnificent dream returned to sing of their death to the wolves.

7/19/76

*1976*

**A DREAM (Version 2 - A SONG FOR WOLVES)**

I sit and wait for dawn's crowning fingers that seem to take their time choking the night. The falsehood of years in the milk bottle of dreams, white dreams clouded over with memory. A dog walks past me wearing the saddle of his beloved father. He is the only son cherished by magnetic diamonds. The seal is broken in water pipes that leak from the heart. The falsification of a lie in a box meant for the dying. The year ended with the dead, for they forgot their smiles. Youth was spent looking for dreams, only from behind a black curtain. There were some ladies who wept on their sleeves and tarnished them. A breaking of the ghost of meticulous fingers poked at the stars. When dawn arrived it devoured ob. I settled myself in its stomach. It was there at the point of dawn that the birds of magnificent dream returned to sing of their death to the wolves.

7/19/76

**PLACID BOAT**

There is a placid boat stealing
Through the clouds of night
Its billows show gaunt swelling
I believe I can call it
Into my living room and change the room into the moon
My face would be metallic
The grimace of fortitude
And developing glass menagerie
And then who invoked
The blackness anyway

7/9/76

## THE RAIN FOREST IS FULL OF RABBITS

There are swallows
Frozen in the refrigerator
That hums to the ham
There are hands
Of lead clouds
Hurrying ahead of the wind
A hungry whale
Proposes to walk
Across a wire
The millipede
Took fair crutches
And flung them in the works
The piano player
Went mad
And broke his mirror
Music continued to resound
Through dead ears
And from pillows.


7/19/76

*1976*

## I AM THE WIDE MOUTH WANDERER

I am the wide mouth wanderer; my face is lead and frost. The glass at my feet flames up. There's a swan that is my face. I am the wind speaking images. My rolling sex migrates with silence upon the strange lights that appear at the edge of my clocks. There are frozen poisons in my eyes and the hands of the dead whisper at my feet.

I am, always the moment before daylight, the hour of the wolf and the moment of slaying pray. My words have not heard black thunder, but touch the white light. I am he who said, you were in fantasy. My fingers grip the clouds. There beyond the bleakness stands the figure of my countenance. Is there any reason not to go further than anyone else?

Is there any reason not to peer deep into the tire treads of my eyes? Perhaps the walls of your room are mirrors in which to pass. My voice reaches you, I'm sure. The crackle of dry leaves gives way to your presence. Is there any reason for you to close your eyes when coming through the door? Perhaps it's the odor of my breath calling out with silver hands. I have eaten roses by the full of the moon. I am not ever running away from you, but walking backward toward you with my heels. You stand as though the earth split you in two. Is that a case of blindness? You resemble the world, crucified by the balls of an automobile. I have gossamer moth wings that smell of honey and mint.

I am the walrus who rushes your door. Have you counted your coins yet, under the bloody portrait of Avida? Watch me from the corner of your eye, I may disappear or let you doubt my visibility. You can take one step, but your step goes backward, not into my waiting glance. Perhaps it's the way you are. You face north and walk east. You walk sideways, never to mindful of the past, but always eyeing the future with compromising eyes. Is this your alleged alliance of a playful dance? Then let me speak to you thoughtfully as if I hadn't in the past. What song do you choose? A light waltz on the edge of a razor? A quick tango with the broken mirrors? Then let it begin with my sweet whispering song. You are gallant for your eyes blaze a fire of someone in the hand of madness. There is no laziness of the wind and the soles of feet leave their owners The glaze of burnt honey covers the sky to obscure the view of my effervescence and my robes of smoke. I am the wide-mouth wanderer.

7/8/76

## VINDICTIVE

Vindictive
>> bird
>>>> space
>>>>>> leaves itself in the
multi-bliss night
>> like thunder
>>>> claws of a hammer
that is the hand stealing
>> last loaves of bread
>>>> and all the swallows migrate
>>>> across the wind
>>>>>> to touch
>>>>>>>> an eyeglass
>>>>>>>>>> folding
>> into what?
the needle in the flesh of time
>> flying by
>>>> on the
>>>>>> wing


7/29/76


## TAKE YOUR HANDS OFF THE WIND

Take your hands off the wind's jealous confection of the air. The roses that are your hands grip with the power of their forgotten faith. Lead eyes caress the sight of such a thing. That is a moment when all the thoughts come forth like bellowing giant sloths, who with angry fingers takes themselves about in the tail of a humming bird. There is no relief to the quake in the forest. It burns in the dawn's light, a light caught in the pupil of the eye.


8/12/76

*1976*

**CRIME OF TEARDROPS**

It is a crime of teardrops
That swiftly takes your buttered hands
Puts them to the lips of dolphins
And caresses the tips of them with wine
The air of your dream takes folds
Is a tourniquet on the neck of a horse?
The dreams of the past woven
Into the fibers of wood the floor
Too is ancient
Reeking of lost moods in the jungle


8/15/76




**FEAR STAINS ON THE WINDOW**

    There are spiders that enter the window through cracks in the moonlight. They keep whispering to the panes of glass that resemble faces. There are voices in the wind that rumble the stones like intimate light. Tears gather in the dust like beads of lips. The spiders crawl into my ears and look at the blind cellars of wine. My fingers are tight around the balls of cities. Cities that resemble hairs of a dog. A dog that is the collar of a society of sweltering madness. The mirror is coated with a fine film of transparent flesh. The spiders that are in the cupboard are speaking secret tongues to the witnesses of the flogging. Their homes were burned during the plague. They caught the disease at the mercy of my teeth. They ran into the corners to seek the dust and roll it into balls. They rolled the balls into my hair and stared at the burning towns. The only fear that was clinging outside resembled that which was on the inside.

8/16/76

## REFLECTIONS IN STAGNANT POOLS

    I gaze past the reflections hidden in the stagnant pools of amorphous voices, voices that call out to me past the fog of my mind. Am I mad, or just contemplating the delicious juices of desire? I let my finger-tips weave a fine transparent film over the holes in the wall. There is no question as to the direction of the voices that come out to haunt me. What can I say to the wind when it comes to greet me? What is your fate? Or to what extent do you greet death's shadows? Run past the rowing window into my palm. You castrated the costumes of clowns. Your half-baked reflection on the glass takes from me the shadows of my breath. Lead me to the trenches that allow me to hide from your wings. I call aloud and I'm frozen in the pillows of dust and fire. See, I say again, there is no revealing consequence as the lever is pulled on the electrocution.

8/17/76


## SPARROWS RIDE THE TRAINS

Who are those naked sons that quibble in the moth's eyes.
The response of a fire is set by the hands of a clock.
A clock that has stolen heaven and stuffed it inside its heart
that ran with the willows to the marsh and dissected their fingers.
The railway has had its tracks uprooted and taken to the caverns.
They are sunk deep into the wounds of a general fallen in his sleep,
bloody with the murdered faces of the peasantry,
who laid the foundation for the last call of beheaded eagles.
They were caught by the breeches and hung by the neck.
There sitting in ruins by a lake full of swans that were caught by the wrist
and their naked lovers were the only exception to the case of the walled
up cats...

8/23/76

*1976*

## CROSS YOUR EYES

Cross your eyes
Urine is in the wind
The men in straightjackets
Seduce the walls
With their sex of iron
Sleeves of brick
Attack the spirit of blood
There are no feelers
From the heads of roaches
That climbed to the top
Of black trees
Apples are roasted
In the same pits
As the cherries
The train that
Is going to Tucker
Is also going to hell

8/24/76

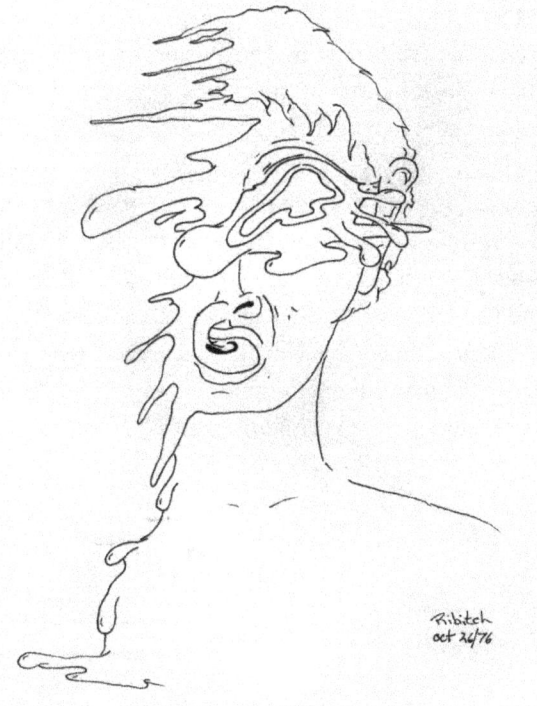

## SONG OF THE WIND
### (the music of John Coltrane)

    I hear the song of the wind as it weeps a mournful tune into my heart. The song of an enchanted gust. The pain of a struggling spirit set on the form of wings. Wings that cannot and will not sit still beyond the touch of the breeze. The swan could not lie still in the rushes, but sprang forth with a lute of magnificent clarity, that broke the chains of the melodious heart, the heart of the swan, the heart that resembled a falcon. The heart of the warm night, picking the blood of the moon. The heart of splendid desire developing the rose of flesh. Hands take apart the mountains to feel the soft intestines of its core. There is a mouth that speaks in screams, screams of the wind, and screams of the whistle of a train. A train whose destination is neither touched by demon or god, but highly developed in the soul of fire. Fire, the wind in your heart. The blessedness of a horn that met death. Death the street reminder that flesh melts beyond your fingers. The sweet tears touch the bellowing sky. A sky full of fire and wind. A sky that is human yet with the ferociousness of a beast. A beast whose eyes roll forward for a glance at certain futures. This is the tear that speaks with a voice of thunder. Blank black whistle in the clouds. A touch of silk in the hand. A dream of hallucinated fish, soft faces full of fingers. Fingers that press the heart and fill it with light and sound. Sounds of the weeping finch sitting on hot glass. Sounds of illusion in the palm of the hand. Sounds of a cricket singing the funeral dirge. There are lips that whisper it to the moon with sounds of footsteps in an empty hallway. Hallways of desire and hallways of blood and tears. Flying through the sun on a horse of ice, on the magical mystery of floating fingers. Fingers that run the rail toward a train of spirit. Spirit, the fire in the black night, lighting the way to the wind. The wind with its song to the clouds, a mournful tune into my heart.

8/24/76

*1976*

**CUTTING THE CLAWS FROM MY SLEEVES**

   The moths of guile take flight in their own amorphous imagination. They take violence by the teeth and whirl the blades on their fingers past the eyes of the fearful priest, whose laughter is benign. The bile on his teeth smells of spoiled milk on the floors of the prison. I took a glass from the closet and broke it in my hand. The pain was the exquisite whisper from the lips of vampires. The glass pierced my flesh like butterflies. I hail torn from the sweet moths into my fingers, wet from their fragrant juices. All the blood that is spilt fills the cups, where lips wait to taste the red sperm of some ancient life. I ask the corners of my room what was the impossible romance between the sleeves of my shirt and the blood of my wrist. I was answered with the oily silence of dumb waiters as they cut with sharpened knives the claws from crabs.

8/30/76

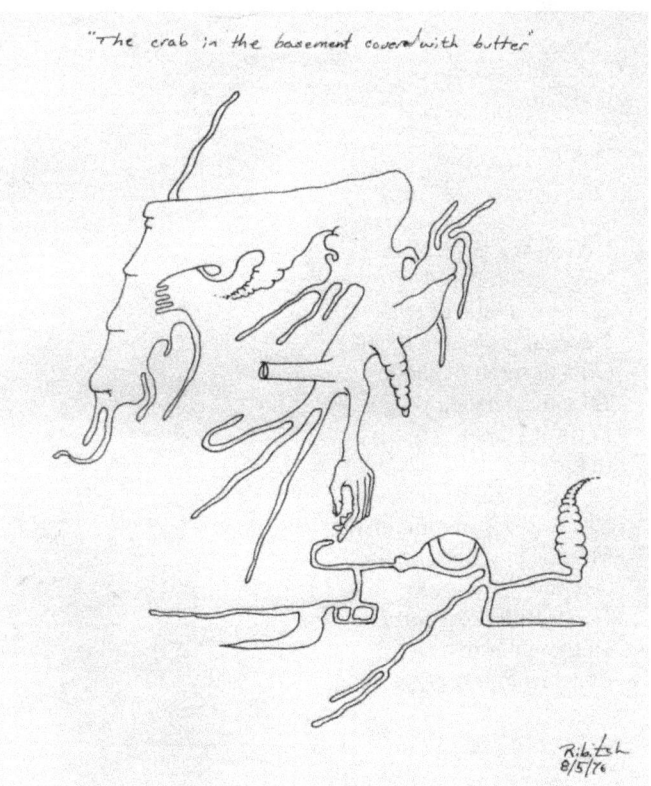

## RIDING ON A GUST OF WIND

Riding on a gust of wind
With pantaloons of silver
The leash about the neck
Of the dog gave notice
To the failing heart
That was the wind
Of Abraxas
There in the bog
The butterflies
That sucked blood
Gathered themselves
Like wolves after dinner
To take the fools
And parade them
Before the picture windows
Of hated violence


8/30/76




## LAKE OF SNAKES

There is a lake of snakes
Revealing like the dawn
On a horizon of sheep
Take their hands
And fold them
In the laps
Of the crazy runners
Caves in the mountainside
Mouths that open to the
Outside
The mouth is an entrance
To the unknown
Beaches of a fire


9/5/76

*1976*

**CARNIVAL**

Place the jabbering unicycle
inside their wooden crates
like coffins in the windows
where monks can look on
in amazement and doubt.
The pikers play charades
in the dark corners
of a burning carnival
where the horses
of the carrousel
look mad and bleed
at the mouth.
The lakes are full
of the drowning
Popes who are made
to look like pigeons
in death.


9/6/76

**THE DAWN IS PLACID**

The dawn is placid
under my feet,
with thorns that
enter my soul
and bleed me.
I am a pain
of fish caught
in the current
of flame.
Naked as I am,
and touched with
the rope of unpleasant memory.
The cascade of hollows
are found in the hands
screwed to the palm
like teardrops.


9/6/76


**EXCLAMATION**

An explosion reeks through the glass
of an old window filled with cobwebs and frost,
to take a look at the sun in its last beating touch.
A cow is born to the virgin.
A birth of crime against the solid wall of smiles in the air.
Then there is an opening that lets in all the wind
and heat to turn cheeks red from embarrassment.


9/25/76

*1976*

**THE ACT OF DRAWING**

Let me speak to you now with the clarity of the spark of the marvelous... Touch your hand to sate the ink flow. Take It now... flow with the pure psychic automatism.

        DRAW!
        DRAW!
        DRAW!
        DRAW!
        DRAW!

9/25/76


**EUPHORIA ERASE ME**

I count the blood on the window.
Euphoria, erase me,
take my lips and press them
into the fabric of the clouds.
Asphyxiate the hand
that grows in the corner,
like the rose under-foot
Ether and smoke,
water from my mouth.
I am wading through the mill
of old forgotten moths.
The glass is broken.
The window is crazy
and has forgotten my name.
Euphoria, erase me,
take my flight and see it burn.

9/26/76

## LET ME LAUGH AFTER YOU

Let me laugh after you
Like a tortoise
Resembling rock
With all the heavens
Watching with netted fingers
Netted in the sky
There is no humor
That beats my hand
That chokes the clouds
I bedevil you
With a sadness
And you don't
Realize it yet
As there is
No fear in your eyes


9/26/76




## ROAD TO THE INFINITE

There is a lake full of swans
that has billfolds of iron.
There is a closet full of screams
that pierces my hand with nails.
The blood that trickles from my palm
sings to me by my bedside.
There is a floor full of lice;
those are diplomats of the dead.
There is a rising face that is a tongue of spiders.
The wall of my mind has crumbled down
and is now a roadway to the infinite.


9/26/76

*1976*

**PAZ**

I'll sit
with your lungs
of fire
the worms
have eaten
though the fog
on desire's throat
manacles of the current
take to the wind
into the blind corners
of a street singer
weeping
as we sit
in the Vicente de Colona
sipping rose
and the flame
of your poetic
fists cry
in the night
viva la revolution
we shall
see the new age and the burning
of false documents.


9/30/76

## POEM FOR SADE

let's explore
the old haunts
of the Marquise de Sade
as he wandered
the sanitarium
before his liver
exploded into
fine fish.

the wedding
of his bath
executed the
last breath
of fall before
it's immersed
itself in winter.

the chains
of the poor devils
were handed
through the bars
of the window
as a plate
front the potash
the hunting
was just beginning.


9/30/76

*1976*

**SMELLS THE NIGHT**

A secret mergence
with myself
can only lead
to the burning
of certain fires
in the halls
of my eyes.
the inner self
shall rip at the outer
with teeth of
razors
and then cast it
from the body
to haunt the sanctums
of brooding silence.
This is an untold fact,
My hand clutches
the visor over dreams,
for I, the dreamer,
am damned
to cross the solstice
in a parade
of leaves.
With light in one
and darkness
in the other,
it is the sadness
of my mind
that reaches
to the folds
in the hampering
morning.
Too much of nothing
to resist,
and always
a cloud of heartbeats
that linger
with the whispers
of the night.
It is there
in the darkness
with all things

*Ribitch: The Last Word, Volume 1*

nocturnal
that I listen
to the pangs
of the coyote
resting in the rushes
with the almost
silent plops of bullfrogs,
that take their flight from
the moon into their own
harsh green darkness

9/30/76

*1976*

## THE APHIDS WILL EAT YOUR FINGERS

There is a garden with dogs blooming in the heat of their mouths, fresh flowers explode in the hand of the ravaging multitude, and canons of bluebells devour the fuchsias with teeth of blades, their razor like remarks take the foot of the gardener and twist him to death beneath the jesting glance of the sunflowers. This is a garden of blood, garden of twisted fates that linger too long under the haze of pandemonium clouds, and there in the garden is the rape of willows, their arms hanging in sorrowful vengeance about the neck of dying citrus. Garden of Sade, perfect violence in the leafy hands eaten by aphids sucked by millipedes in their hungry search for the juices of malignant death, death in the wrinkled gray of decomposition, morbid as youth poisoned in the marsh.

9/30/76

## INTO THE CELLAR

The caretaker took my hand
and blows cheese into it
with a smile
flavored with arsenic.
The flavor of a mint tongue
wipes the glass
of its dust,
and takes it and
savors the wind
with gold blood
and wine.
The cooks have taken wind
and made soup
of their smiles.
There are maids
in the cellar
who are chained?
and wiped bloody
with their own skirts.

10/13/76

## THE PREMATURE WISHING OF THE FROZEN

While giving up the notion of the fact
While pretending that the fleet of roses
Takes from its mouth a violent urge
It is only fair to resume our walk
With our tongues to the dark places in the hall
The things that are recounted as the infinite
Take trains to Lisbon to wait
In respect for challenging us to utter
The silence of lions
There are no more felt hats
Laid astrew on the ice
Thin and cracked with the weathered
Blows of the rain beckoning
With soft whispers for diligent hands
To beat, unmercifully, a priest
Who resemble the dogs of an untamed alley
Is that why the city turns red
Under its blistering hate
It tongue bubbled with disease
The throat of its madness
Taken for a ride along the avenues
Of stilted desire those hats resemble coffins
Is not for me to answer
But to take with my eye
The explosions of revolt
In the halls of social complaint
The wavering promise of guilt
Plays the role sickness
At the feet of desire
It is true that my hand
Has murdered a bird singing outside
As it sat on a limb like a frozen torso
In the glimpse of a convulsion
I can admit that what awaits me
Is not of the same flesh
But an illusion on the tip of my tongue
I shall take a match and set fire
To the curtains so that they will at last
Reveal to me the pleasures
That wait beyond the soot-covered windows

11/2/76

*1976*

## CROWN OF MAGGOTS

The crown of maggots
distilled in the eyes,
his craw broken
through a megaton
of rose flesh
that homely garden
of runaway fingers
takes its time
on the doubt
of faces
lingered wizened
breath
a lake full of
jackasses
each with
a web foot
calls to crows
in their flight
into bottles.


11/28/76

## A SNAKE IS YOUR PET, WARM BLANKET

I spent half my life
chasing the dust
that sticks to my eyelids.
My heartbeat
strokes the beak
of some strange idea
that is a lesson
of unfolding walrus tusk.
The animals of transfiguration
seal the bonds
of air that is ptomained.
I vomit the jealousies
that were spent by my father
on his last trip to a seizure.
The heart burst
like a fountain pen
leaving ink
on the bird's wing.
A day that is classified
erupting the bones
of day for the
mouths to speak.


11/30/76

*1976*

**RED MACKEREL**

guess which hallways
the stolen bananas came from
as they stand on the chest
of a red mackerel
the haunting reminiscent
foliage appears to be
the beard of a dead man
his features resemble
the climate insofar
as the clouds
are buried in
the hollows of the hand,
the hand that bleeds mercury
and tiny birds
of walrus


11/30/76


**THE DISASTER OF 1910**

The air that surrounds me is milk,
its white leaves touching
me like wire.
A hot taste in my eye
resembles birdshit.
A hungry tortoise
visited my grandfather's grave
to tell him he was
a mongoose with wings.
Salt etches a white circle
above the tombs
of silent aborigines
their tongues folded back
in a defiant gust
of cranial farts.


11/30/76

## HEIRLOOM

I walked into the room
and was taken by the hand
by a chair.
The formed wood sitting piece
took me to Babylon
and showed me the
streams of blood
that spoke in a language
I could not recognize.
They had double-knit
mouths with blood stains
of the crimes of the state
that is visited upon
by the son
and imposed upon by the daughter
and laid to rest
by the family heirloom of pride.


12/2/76


## SECRET DOCUMENTS

Take the spiders out of your mouth
they itch your tongue
with wet mops.
A toilet for gentlemen
whose ears have migrated
to the sun's birth.
Your skin has fallen off,
to be used as parchment
of secret documents.


12/2/76

*1976*

**SWINGING CHERRIES**

Later is the year of
cyclopean fires
that will ride the
wild taste of the wind.
It is a place
of forest fires.
The lips peel.
The lips walk away.
The lips run to
the fall of the house of Usher.

There is a forest
of beast
that wears keys
on their tongues
and baskets in
their hair.
The maker of ribbons
that hung the poor child
in the closet
swings back and forth,
back and forth,
back and forth,
like cherries in the wind.


12/2/76

## LAKE OF FACES

Lake of faces
their lust is complete
in the foam
of a cycle.
The arms outstretched
into the fires of
a deep abyss
that is the eyes of
a lake,
a lake of faces
that ponders
over the death
of roses
on their thin shore.


12/6/76

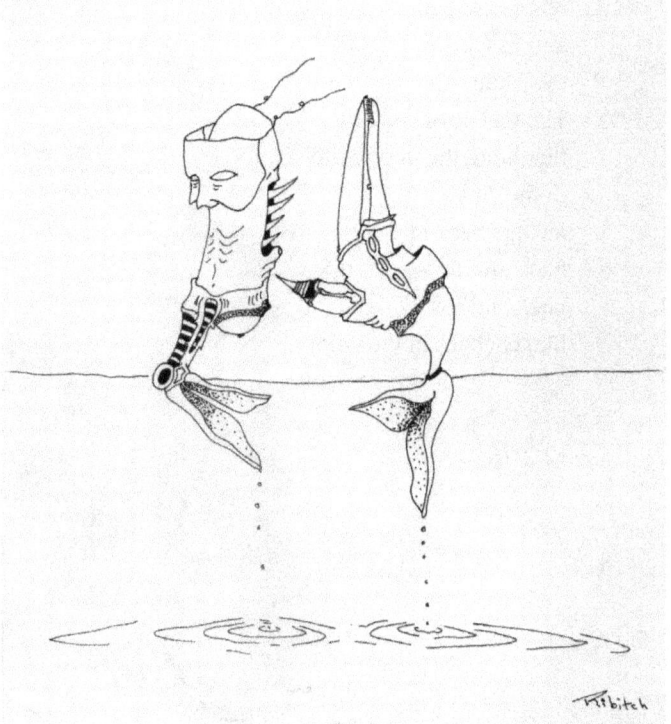

*1976*

**EYES OF COMPLETE DARKNESS**

Eyes of complete darkness
that fills in the earth
with a swallow's hand
is decked out in a holiday
blood wedding dress
that was a glass
cracked in a rage.

To many forest
breath of tongues
with their eyes
is it believable
to stand halfway
between the dead
and the holy ghost?

The desk has taken
away their homely mothers
and executed them
with electric cords


12/7/76

**JAZZ**

I have touched your
eyelids with caterpillars
that are phosphorescent
and flaming blood.
Flowers of sweat
they march to the walls
in their underwear
wearing glasses
of frost.

Crescendos of music
take from the response
a naked birdwing,
strip it, eat it with teeth
of mush, with teeth of tigers
turned to milk.
They can't see themselves,
for they are blind
with the galaxy
writing before them.


12/7/76

*1976*

**A BOAT FULL OF MOLLUSK**

Infinitely grappling with the claws of a baby
who rose from its crib scratching the last
ounce of the wind.
Tearing from my chest a book full of clocks,
a heart full of wind and a violent kind
that uproots trees and sends them
to the devil's paradise with a set of keys
that will lock up their hunger.
The walls of mythos are crumbling
with the foul breath of tortured glass marbles
weighted in their hands to take it all from the forest.
Breaking a wrist watch with a mallet
worn on both ends like the flinching torsos of wolves.
The animal eyes rest in the sockets of somebody's chest.
They are not fools that matter, picturesque,
their tongues heated, their breasts headed once before the light
dawned on a fishbowl of held in violence.
Stakes could not be put through the chest of wooden vampires,
for night had regained its right once again
leaving heavy breath to stale the air.
My arms heavy as the last boat that dredged
the dead mollusk from under his warm blankets,
to steal the fire that was lit in the bowels of his brain.
All the boats that carry the corpora across canals of fever
have been waylaid to pay tax on their bones.
A rock is lighter than feathers breathing a last breath beneath the earth.
The stone trembles at a strange disbelief or a continuous humor.

12/8/76

## THE PILLOW

Inside of a gossamer bag
a pillow is held captive
from its memoirs.
Messages brought by pigeons
wilt with sick bag humor.
Sand crabs hustle
on 5th Ave. for meals of leprosy.
Inside a gossamer bag
a pillow stands raped
by the sheets.
Tears stand gray
on walls of silt.
Rain fears the sun's embrace.
Inside of a gossamer bag
a pillow is taken
for a ride
by things that
won't release it.


12/9/76

*1976*

**DOLLS**

The binding consequence
of dolls with fictitious arms,
they march two by two
up the hills toward
uncertain futures.
The towers that wait for
a scream from the dolls
have a clock
that is feverous
and covered with flies.
The rancor of
its possibilities
haunts the cleaned
breakfast table
touching its sleeve
with the hot breath
of a thousand years
of blindness
inside the booth,
inside the Marker
of Intelligent romance.


12/10/76

## CRIES AND WHISPERS

Someone committed suicide
under a neon light
where the last pretensions
of life had escaped.

The walls of tears
torn from the body
and he wailed in the night.

A diamond was scratching
the inner eyelid
to create a fusion
of breath.

All of the feelers
of insects search
the room,
smelling its death
that lingers thick
like mucus.

Music still plays
though ears have
been pierced of their drums.
Silence, please
the dead are in slumber
and cry loneliness.


12/11/76

*1976*

**SEVERAL TIMES A YEAR**

Several times a year
death waits
with its horns
piercing the sun.
Blood lips and
fingers crooked
up the vaginal
process of life.
Who could stink worse,
them or this impossible mystery?
Is this stale bread
broken by unholy hands?
The phallus erectus
piercing the mouth
of vomiting dreamers,
filling them with
the sperm of nightmare,
filling them with
the hope of the impregnation of ice.
Death walking with a cane
bent over
in humble disguise,
fooling only the few
who tremble before dust.
I cannot falter
in its wake
or its obscene lust
that seems to quake
the earth with
such horrible mythologies.
I grapple with the intent
to make myself know
that I bend the saber
with my teeth
that has been sharpened
for just for such a cause,
for just such an instance
that takes me off guard.
Death handed me
a bouquet of roses
freshened in poison.
Its fragrance

doubling in my nostrils,
but I refused
to partake of its odor,
not by fear
of its hidden valleys
but of defiance
to succumb to
its established order.
Oh, I shall enter voluntarily
the darkened hallways
of amorphous voices,
but only at my choosing,
for I do not carry
death's timepiece
but my own,
which it is my power
to stop or
let unwind
its translucent time.
I feel no anticipation
of the wait
for it is at my own choosing
but to leave death
turning red with frustration
at the futility of
his useless quests,
and his sorry game
to elude me
into the folds
of his desire.

12/11/16

*1976*

**A LOCKET SHAPED LIKE A HEART**

I put a respirator
inside a locket shaped
like a heart.
It was for lovers only
who were feverish
and made of glass.
I don't know
how many spaces
there were in the wind
but it almost
cleared the top
of the stairs
and saw to it
that all the stories
were the ease of,
the same lines,
the same eyes.
        It was…


12/15/76

## ALL BUT THE NIGHT

All but the night
singing in my hands,
taking birds from
my eyes
and enveloping desire
with the wings of fish.
The sweet whispers
of angels
thrown from their heaven,
consumed in the fire
that cut through to me
on the other side
of the window.
To call all but the night,
all but the night
wearing the moon on its sleeve.
Pressing itself upright
to breathe again that of rhinoceros.
All but the night
slumbers in pleasantries
their desires.
The wind is caught up in the turmoil
of the jealous night.
To sing all but the night,
with its claws dug deep
into the eyes of a star-watcher's belly,
ripped open leaving an empty carcass in it black waste.
All but the night with silver pearls
and its notes of death.
All but the night has closed its doors
and now sits waiting to pounce on dreamers
to take their sleep to sew their eyes shut.
All but the night, all but the night
swallows itself in a handful of thorns.

12/15/76

*1976*

**HOUSE OF HORNS**

On the horns of a jackal
I am feverishly riding
a somnambulant wind
with a saber.
Castles of coffins
made of the red clay of your sex,
because the laid-bare floors of rooms
are swallows taking themselves
to the heights of a whisper.
Leaving alone a picture of the rain,
they finish themselves
covered with pearls,
that too, is the way of the lion,
the way of the lust,
the climbing of the birds on the vine.


12/15/76

## RESPIRATOR

I put a respirator
inside a locket shaped
like a heart.
It was for lovers only
who were feverish
and made of glass.
I don't know
how many spaces
there were in the wind
but it almost
cleared the top
of the stairs
and saw to it
that all the stories
were the same,
same lines,
same eyes,
it was...


12/15/76

*1976*

**WALLS**

The walls that fill disgrace with fingers
are worn from their hermetic duties.
The criminal generals
walk with padded footsteps,
like lions blowing horns,
like the claws of a mouse
seeking entrance into the heart
of a terrible beast.
A beast whose intention
is to erupt the blood vessels
that connect the eyes
to the filaments of desire.
The graveyard of many sorrows
uphold the pleasures
of Eros waiting by the curb
in the essence of thought.


12/16/76

## I CARRIED MYSELF IN A BASKET
## THROUGH THE STREETS OF PLAGUE

I carried myself in a basket
through the streets of plague.
The eyes that met mine
were from another time.
They screamed an entrance
I could not give.
Eyes popped from faces
as hunger released
its folds into my hands.
I could feel the hairs
on the back of my neck
respond to the airs of blackness.

I carried myself in a basket
through the streets of plague.
Whispers lent their ears
to the moans of the maimed.
Fear in the air was thick
and could only be pierced
with wedding swords.
The drumming of the dead
in their cloaks of spiderwebs
haunted the stillness like a knife.
The day was dreary with
the burning.

I carried myself in a basket
through the streets of plague.
To the house of the priest,
that was locked and barred with iron.
The bells in the towers
gave toll to the succumtion.
Flowers of the wind
gave breath to the foray of men,
who quibbled over
the expense of the night.
Laughter in the rafters,
that fire burned the bodies
made of cotton and tears.

*1976*

I carried myself in a basket
through the streets of plague.
In the marketplace
where meat hung rotting, a gift to flies,
and wagons went thumping
over cobblestones smeared with blood.
At the end of streets bodies piled
marked by a cross hung dummy,
cloaked in black
giving warning to the stench
of burnt flesh.
The calls of the mourners
rasping in the night
with callused throats.

I carried myself in a basket
through the streets of plague.
I taunt the jealousies of the elite,
hidden in their stone wombs,
prisoners of their fates.
Stonewalls of blackness.
The ink of hearts
Bleeding on blistered feet.
The ships have come in
with the rats of unholy disease.
That merchants arrive
with pockets full of bent coins
worth nothing to the soulless dead
whose nameless misfortunes
cast their weight in the undertaker's palm.

I carried myself in a basket
through the streets of plague
singing the song of the funeral dirge
to witness a birth at the foot of the pyre.
Horses stinking,
their asses milky with disease.
Flies converse from nostril to nostril
laying the seed of their obscene maggots
in the sockets of eyes.
Babies cried alone,
their tongues swollen and cracked

## Ribitch: The Last Word, Volume 1

outside the doors of their homes
that were marked with the sign of death.

I carried myself in a basket
through the streets of plague
with no light in my eyes
for it is lost in the darkness
of hearts severed from the chest
spilling life for the dogs
to lap up with their pointed tongues.
Displaced fear strangles all hope
that may be left hanging in corners full of webs.

I carried myself in a basket
Through the streets of plague
carrying red banners and field of roses,
crying to squires and rag peasants.
Their hands never touch mine.
Never, nothing so dreadful
as to claim so many
as this death curse of darkness
unfolding the ribbons of fear
and so with blood caked
beneath my fingernails,
whispering the secrets of blackness,
lips swollen from fire,
I carried myself in a basket
through the streets of plague.

12/18/76

*1976*

## BIRTH OF JACKKNIVES

What description could I give
for rabbit hole eyes,
a white robe
of smoke,
a spear of butter
haunting the depth
of a heart,
the craven walls
called mythos
torn from my hands,
giving liberty
to a birth of jackknives

12/30/76

**PARACHUTES**

There is silk in proportion
to the wires of wind
that also is leaving tracks
in the dust for hermaphrodites
to follow
Knowing the full intent of
the ravenous sea
that stands on a table
made of bones
We can mark the end
of time in a few
measurable amounts
of a horse beaten
by a pile of machinery
The fork is stuck
through a tongue
so it cannot speak
out the words of iron,
the words of smoke,
or the cross between
that takes it so long
to develop a paradise


12/30/76

*1976*

## THE CLOUDS OF YOUR WANING HAIR

The clouds of your waning hair
wait for the dawn
to count its fingers.
The chalk of Wizards
roams the hallways of your eyes
in search of paralyzing
moments of lizard umbrellas.
Making a frost of jealousies
that tints the air
with a color of water lips.
The nakedness of an ashcan
croons the belly of saving machines
slumbering on the banks
of shivering moons.

12/30/76

## HATS ON THE RAILWAY

Hats stand on the railroad tracks
as tribute to their sublime actions
voices that are theirs
that are the singing of revolt.

The hats brandish red stains
in the palms of hands whose fortunes
can't be told for the sharp clap of thunder
between the gravel and the rail.

The fact that there are hats on the railway
gives note to the explosion of trains.

12/31/76

## MY SLEEP IS INTERRUPTED

My sleep is guided
by drops of water
wanted by the gray eyes
of hard vegetables
mountains maintain
their watch over the obsolete
figurations of dolls
with arms of mummies
with arms of granite
here in their frost pools
eyes sink into lips
bloody with the frost
taken back into the cross section
of joyous
breathing rocks


12/31/76




## THE DUST OF NEW HAMPSHIRE

The dust of New Hampshire
settles on the eyelids
of any new frosted dawn
It is as nobody knew before
limestone graves
and windows of stone
listening to the footsteps
of trees
the voices of the earth
that murder the townspeople
with its leaven razors
of soft cream


12/31/76

# About The Author:

Ribitch (Rib-Itch): A scratch on the rib, or something that bothers you. The name is a play on words and a bit of Humor Noir. For all of his life, Samuel Martin Ribitch had an affinity for surrealism and was an active member of the International Surrealist Movement. Since his introduction to Philip Lamantia and the Bay Area Surrealist Group in 1975 he had been involved in several major Surrealist exhibitions. Soon after this momentous meeting he travelled to Chicago to meet with the Arsenal Group and attended *The World Surrealist Exhibition: Marvelous Freedom, The Vigilance of Desire*. Over 33 Nations were represented, showing the solidarity of all the individual groups worldwide. In 1978 Ribitch returned to Chicago and helped organize another International surrealist exhibit: *The 100th Anniversary of Hysteria*.

Ribitch collaborated and communed with surrealist comrades from around the world. He exhibited in several group shows and also had his own solo exhibitions. He published two chapbooks of poetry (*Nefftania* and *Third Morning*) as well as a full-length volume of poetry, *Carnival of Sleep* (Oyster Moon Press), and then co-edited the literary journal *Somanmbulist* with fellow surrealist Sharon Olson. His work was also published in *Surrealism and Its Popular Accomplices* (Cultural Correspondence), *Free Spirits* (City Lights), *The Somnambulist Footprints* and *Hydrolith* (Oyster Moon Press), and most recently in the first bilingual edition of *Analogon*, the journal of the Surrealist Movement in Prague.

Ribitch's views of surrealism can be summed up in his own words: "It is a lightning field of the possible, where the horizon is set aflame by human potential. It is here amongst the corellas of this possibility that the marvelous displays its fine wings of gossamer silk and smoke. It is the play between the invisible and the visible dancing under a moon, recognizing its dreams in crystalline reflection. It is the erotic sensation of a breath, like the shaman's drum, the heartbeat of the marvelous calling to the unseen chimeras of the unconscious to reveal their stories at the edge of the eye."

# OYSTER MOON PRESS

***The Mountains of Mourne***, by Séamas Cain (2019). A collection of poems in English written over the course of 60 years, published in February of 2019. With eight photographs by Gloria DeFilipps Brush, marking the different sections of poems. 182 pages.

***Out of Odessa and Into Ideation***, by Eric Bragg (2017). A collection of automatic texts and stories spanning the years 2002–2013: fully intoxicated with cunning sarcasm, social commentary and the erotic, totally "licking you with my thoughts and thinking of you with my tongue." 292 pages.

***The Audiographic As Data***, by Will Alexander & Carlos Lara (2016). The Audiographic As Data is none other than telepathic conundrum. It is language that renders the visible as invisible and the invisible as visible thus, transmuting both states into incalculable presence. 92 pages.

***Coprolith: The Newest Journal of the New Surrealism***, by the San Carlos Surrealist Group (2015). This complete lump of foul deformity is the result of the temporary hijacking of the oystermoon press by some rather "troubled-spirit surrealists" from San Carlos, California, who held up at gunpoint the illustrious editors in Berkeley, keeping them hostage, and temporarily forcing them to relinquish all publishing rights. If anyone happens to come across any copies of this thoroughly piece-o-shit book, then he or she is advised to immediately incinerate them, and focus instead on the highly esteemed volumes of *Hydrolith*. So as it were, Coprolith might for a short while have been the proverbial "turd in the punchbowl", but nevertheless by now this little problem has been fully rectified. 220 pages.

***Hydrolith 2: Surrealist Research & Investigations*** (2014). This second issue of *Hydrolith* is a continuation of what the first volume started, which was and is to assemble a stimulating selection of exclusively recent work by groups and individuals of the international Surrealist movement, to facilitate intellectual exchange and collaboration, enabling us to concentrate the echoes of our commonalities as well as the shadows of our differences. In so doing, this volume aspires to reduce all manner of distances that exist between us. 368 pages.

**Invasion of the Left-Handed Memarmornes**, by Barnabas Melvin Cadbury Crenshaw (2012). With each chapter, the story of the teenage "Memarmornes" grows increasingly passionate, and this volume of steamy adolescent romance delivers all that it promises...and more. While Mr. Crenshaw's astonishingly limber voice still moves effortlessly between Peter's and Sarah's turbulent relationship and Michael Jackson's growing clairvoyance, from erotic exuberance to more interpersonal gravity, *Invasion of the Left-Handed Memarmornes* is, for the most part, a titillating book that marks the young protagonists' final initiation into the excesses and discrepancies of adulthood. 112 pages.

**Mirach Speaks to His Grammatical Transparents**, by Will Alexander (2011). A philosophical meditation vertically scripted. It is an extension of Alexander's first book in this mode, Towards The Primeval Lightning Field. Both books in concert, exist as a double exploration, in what, for the author, is a nascent odyssey, concerning the mind at non-limit through cellular transmogrification. 152 pages.

**Carnival of Sleep**, by Ribitch (2011). Between dream and hallucination, *Carnival of Sleep* opens its tent for the unwary somnambulist. Ribitch's prose and poetry are sometimes dark and humorous, sometimes sublime lamentations of erotic beauty and deeply surrealist in storytelling. They are like ruptured blood vessels, gushing forth a spray of blood droplets, each bearing a different face. Illustrations by the Author. 180 pages.

**West of Pure Evil**, by Josie Malinowski (2010). The labyrinthine, mercurial worlds of Josie Malinowski's *West of Pure Evil* represent a divorce between rhyme and reason, spinning off-key tales of love and pain. Sailors and whores unite to solve ancient, despicable mysteries; an act of aid brings a Fairy Kingdom to its knees; and the tragic Captain Cock is left cold and stiff by a scheming eight-year-old. These myriad poems and stories illuminate the crossover between waking and dreaming, and thereby cast an intimate, surrealist glance at the human condition. 204 pages.

**Hydrolith: Surrealist Research & Investigations** (2009). *Hydrolith* brings together in one volume some of the most exciting recent work from the international surrealist movement. With over 80 contributors from 17 countries around the world, the book contains drawings, paintings, games, comics, photographs, poetry, prose, theoretical and political writings on a huge variety of subjects, including special in-depth investigations of music, space and myth. The book is a must-read for anyone interested in the surrealist movement today. 240 pages.

***The Exteriority Crisis*** (2008). In its corners, streets, gates, bars, squares, boulevards, gardens, parks and cafés, the city maintains some of the focal points of "its" unconscious. These are found and explored everyday by surrealists who obtain the essential experience of surreality in metropolitan life. The concrete experience of exteriority (which in the following collective essay we concentrate only on the city limits and beyond them) requires from us a disposition closely akin not only to the sensible renewal of people, but also to existence and its poetic reserves, and to the revitalization of the interior life that is suffering a process of sterilization because of the convulsive technologization of interiority and the progressive forgetting of life outside. 184 pages.

***The Somnambulist Footprints*** (2008). The result of a collective project in which several contemporary surrealists and fellow travelers wrote short stories according to their own interests and imperatives, based on their common desire to subvert the very foundations of conventional reality, both on the written page and – more importantly – beyond it, in the open space of consciousness. Contributing authors: Mariela Arzadun, J. Karl Bogartte, Daniel Boyer, Eric W. Bragg, Mattias Forshage, Parry Harnden, Dale Michael Houstman, Philip Kane, Merl, Ribitch, Matthew Rounsville, Shibek, Andrew Torch, and Xtian. 216 pages.

***The Midnight Blade of Sonic Honey*** (2008). The pairing of a surrealist novel and an automatic text by Eric W. Bragg (www.surrealcoconut.com), that were written nearly seven years apart but which tell the same story, albeit as complementary permutations of each other. Dripping with bile and centered within a gothic sensibility, this journey opens the reader's skull like a freshly cracked coconut. With illustrations by Ribitch (www.ribitch.net). 236 pages.

Oyster Moon Press is a non-profit, surrealist publishing co-op located in Berkeley, California.

If you're after individual copies, you can find our titles online at places like Lulu, Amazon, Barnes & Noble, and Borders.

If you are a bookstore, then you can make bulk orders through our distributor, Small Press Distribution (SPD) books.

OYSTER
MOON
PRESS

www.ingramcontent.com/pod-product-compliance
Lightning Source LLC
Chambersburg PA
CBHW022100150426
43195CB00008B/211